QANON

QANON

QUINN SILVER

CONTENTS

Introduction: The Rise of a Conspiracy

In October 2017, an anonymous account with the name "Q" began posting cryptic messages on the imageboard 4chan, a forum well-known for its anonymity and subversive content. The initial posts claimed that high-ranking government officials and global elites were involved in an intricate web of child trafficking, Satanic rituals, and corruption. At the center of this conspiracy, according to "Q," was a shadowy cabal of powerful figures who not only controlled the world's financial and political systems but also orchestrated heinous crimes involving children. On the opposing side, Q portrayed then-President Donald Trump as a messianic figure who was secretly battling this evil cabal from within the highest echelons of power.

This was the beginning of what would become one of the most widely known and controversial conspiracy theories of the 21st century: QAnon.

The Central Claim: A Global Cabal

QAnon's central belief is that a secret cabal of Satan-worshipping pedophiles, including many powerful politicians, celebrities, and business leaders, controls not only the United States but the world. This group is said to be involved in a vast, underground network of human trafficking, harvesting adrenochrome—a chemical compound that QAnon believers claim is derived from children's blood—as part of their sinister activities. These elites, according to QAnon, operate within the shadows, using their wealth and influence to manipulate political systems, orchestrate wars, and control global events for their gain.

The idea of a secret, all-powerful group controlling the world is not new. Conspiracy theories about shadowy elites have existed for centuries, from anti-Semitic tropes like The Protocols of the Elders of Zion to Cold War paranoia about secret communist agents. What sets QAnon apart is its timing, its digital origins, and the way it merges various conspiracy theories into one overarching narrative. Unlike previous conspiracy theories that remained in fringe publications or the dark corners of the internet, QAnon spread rapidly across social media platforms, gaining millions of followers who saw themselves as part of a "Great Awakening" to expose this cabal.

The Role of Donald Trump

Central to QAnon is the belief that Donald Trump is not only aware of the existence of this cabal but that he is waging a secret war against them. To QAnon followers, Trump's presidency was not just another chapter in American politics—it was a pivotal moment in the battle between good and evil. They believed that Trump's often unconventional and erratic behavior was part of a larger plan, carefully orchestrated to dismantle the deep state and bring justice to the cabal members. In their eyes, Trump's cryptic tweets and offhand remarks were not political missteps but encoded messages intended to communicate with those "in the know."

QAnon followers also latched onto the notion that Trump was working in tandem with the U.S. military to stage a great counterattack, culminating in "The Storm"—a day when high-profile cabal members would be arrested en masse, tried, and executed. This belief stems from a Trump comment in October 2017, when he told reporters that a gathering of top military officials represented "the calm before the storm." When asked to clarify, Trump smiled and said, "You'll find out." To QAnon believers, this was clear confirmation that Trump was signaling the beginning of the end for the global cabal.

The Q Drops

"Q" communicated with followers primarily through cryptic posts called "Q drops." These drops consisted of a mix of coded language, military jargon, and conspiracy-laden hints. Q's posts would often challenge followers to "do the research" and connect the dots themselves, creating an engaging, almost game-like atmosphere where followers could work together to decode the "truth." This sense of participatory discovery helped build a community of dedicated believers, who saw themselves as "digital soldiers" fighting to expose the cabal.

The Q drops were vague enough to be interpreted in many ways, which helped keep followers engaged. Even when predictions made in Q drops failed to materialize, followers found ways to rationalize the discrepancies. For example, when predictions about mass arrests of prominent political figures or the revelation of secret indictments didn't happen, QAnon believers would claim that the timeline had shifted or that disinformation was necessary to confuse the enemy. In this way, QAnon created a self-sustaining feedback loop, where failed predictions only deepened believers' resolve and dedication.

The Rapid Spread of QAnon

While QAnon began on the fringes of the internet, its growth was exponential, thanks in large part to social media platforms like Facebook, Twitter, and YouTube. What started as a niche community on 4chan quickly found its way into mainstream social media, where algorithms that favored sensational content helped spread QAnon theories to a much wider audience.

One of the reasons for QAnon's rapid spread was its ability to absorb other conspiracy theories. It acted like a conspiracy theory vacuum, pulling in ideas from other fringe movements—everything from anti-vaccine rhetoric to flat-earth theories to fears about 5G technology. This adaptability made QAnon appealing to a wide range of people, from political extremists to concerned parents worried about child trafficking.

As the movement grew, it began to attract the attention of mainstream media and political figures. Some Republican politicians and candidates for office openly embraced QAnon, using its ideas to mobilize a base of disaffected voters. This gave the movement a veneer of legitimacy in the eyes of some followers, further fueling its growth.

The Role of Social and Political Disillusionment

The rise of QAnon cannot be separated from the larger political and social context in which it emerged. The years leading up to 2017 were marked by increasing political polarization, economic uncertainty, and distrust in traditional institutions. Many Americans felt left behind by a political system that seemed to serve only the elites, while the media and government appeared to ignore their concerns.

In this environment, QAnon provided an alternative narrative that explained the chaos and division in the world. For many, it was easier to believe that a secret cabal was pulling the strings than to grapple with the more complex realities of economic inequality, global power shifts, and changing cultural norms. QAnon offered a simple, black-and-white worldview: good versus evil, with clear heroes and villains. For those who felt disenfranchised, QAnon was not just a conspiracy theory—it was a form of empowerment.

From Fringe to Mainstream

By 2020, QAnon had moved from an obscure internet conspiracy to a full-fledged social and political movement. It wasn't just discussed on anonymous message boards anymore; it was showing up in mainstream media, at political rallies, and even in conversations with friends and family. QAnon merchandise appeared at Trump rallies, and "Where We Go One, We Go All" (WWG1WGA), a slogan associated with QAnon, became a rallying cry for a segment of Trump supporters.

The COVID-19 pandemic further accelerated QAnon's growth. As people spent more time online, they were exposed to an increasing amount of QAnon content. The pandemic also created fertile ground for conspiracy theories, as people looked for explanations and scapegoats for the global crisis. QAnon filled this void by claiming that the pandemic was either a hoax or part of the cabal's plan to control the population through fear and lockdowns.

Setting the Stage

The rise of QAnon represents a convergence of several societal trends: the erosion of trust in institutions, the power of social media to amplify fringe ideas, and the appeal of simple explanations for complex problems. In the chapters that follow, we will dive deeper into the origins of QAnon, the psychological and social factors driving its appeal, the political implications of its rise, and the personal stories of those affected by the conspiracy.

By understanding how and why QAnon gained traction, we can begin to unravel the broader forces shaping this era of disinformation, distrust, and division. The story of QAnon is not just about one conspiracy theory—it's about the power of belief, the fragility of truth, and the future of democracy in the digital age.

Chapter 1: The Origins of QAnon

1. The Digital Birth: 4chan, 8chan, and Anonymous Message Boards

In October 2017, a series of cryptic posts began appearing on 4chan, an anonymous message board infamous for its anything-goes environment. This new figure, identifying themselves as "Q," claimed to have high-level government security clearance—specifically, "Q-level" clearance, typically reserved for those working with nuclear energy within the U.S. Department of Energy. These posts, referred to as "Q drops," were unlike the usual conspiracy theories that floated around 4chan. They contained puzzling phrases, cryptic questions, and vague assertions that seemed to point to a hidden world of corruption and evil at the highest levels of power. Followers were encouraged to "follow the breadcrumbs" and uncover the secrets of an elite, global cabal allegedly trafficking children and worshipping Satan, with Donald Trump supposedly waging a covert war against them.

Q's arrival on 4chan marked a shift from conspiracy theories that existed primarily in fringe communities to one that quickly spread across multiple platforms and gained a significant following. To understand why Q's messages spread so effectively, it's essential to grasp the culture of 4chan and, later, 8chan—both anonymous message boards where almost anything could be posted and discussed, no matter how bizarre or offensive. These platforms had long served as breeding grounds for internet subcultures, trolling campaigns, and, in some cases, radical ideologies. They offered users a sense of freedom and anonymity not found on mainstream social media sites, which often censor or moderate content. The lack of oversight allowed users to express extreme ideas and conspiracy theories without consequence, creating fertile ground for Q's drops to take root and spread.

4chan's anonymous structure fostered a unique environment where people could interact without the typical social norms or personal accountability seen on sites like Facebook or Twitter. Users were identified only by randomly generated ID numbers, allowing ideas to stand independently of the identities behind them. In the context of QAnon, this anonymity gave Q an air of mystery and credibility. Since no one knew who Q was, followers were free to project their own ideas and beliefs onto the figure, creating a sense of trust and intrigue. Was Q a high-ranking military official? A government whistleblower? Or maybe even Trump himself? The mystery surrounding Q's identity became part of the allure, drawing curious users into the puzzle.

The style of Q's posts was intentionally cryptic. Rather than directly stating information, Q would pose questions or make vague statements, leaving it up to followers to "do the research" and connect the dots. A typical Q drop might read something like: "Who controls the narrative? Who really owns the media? Think mirror. The end will not be for everyone." This style of communication appealed to the user base on 4chan and 8chan, where conspiracy theories and "alternative research" were already popular. The posts encouraged users to engage in a form of gamified investigation, piecing together clues, comparing notes, and feeling as if they were part of an elite group uncovering hidden truths.

As Q's popularity grew, the movement migrated to 8chan, a platform even less moderated than 4chan and notorious for its free-speech absolutism. On 8chan, Q continued to drop clues while building a mythos around a world teetering on the edge of chaos and deception. Here, followers dubbed themselves "anons" and collaborated on "baking" Q's cryptic posts into coherent theories. Each Q drop was treated as a valuable piece of intelligence, dissected and discussed in massive threads as users attempted to unravel what they believed were government secrets. This group investigation process further solidified QAnon's appeal: it was no longer just one person making claims but a community working together to uncover "truth."

This collective experience transformed QAnon into a community-driven movement. Members took pride in their identity as "digital soldiers," and for many, the hunt for truth felt like a heroic mission. They believed they were the only ones who could see the reality hidden beneath the surface, the last bastions of truth in a world of deception. As Q spread its wings across the internet, the movement's initial obscurity on 4chan and 8chan would serve as the foundation for what was to become one of the most significant conspiracy theories of the 21st century. In the world of QAnon, anonymity wasn't a drawback; it was a powerful tool that allowed Q's messages to gain traction, foster devotion, and spread far beyond the fringes of the web.

2. Who is "Q"? The Anonymous Insider

One of the most compelling aspects of the QAnon movement is the mysterious figure at its center—"Q." In a world dominated by social media influencers and personalities, Q was different. No one knew who Q was, and that was precisely the point. This enigmatic figure claimed to have "Q-level" security clearance, a real designation within the U.S. Department of Energy that allows access to top-secret information, usually related to nuclear technology. By adopting this title, Q implied they were a high-ranking government insider with access to classified details far beyond the public's knowledge.

For followers, Q was not just a whistleblower; they were a patriot with insider knowledge of a hidden war between good and evil. According to the posts, this war pitted Donald Trump and his allies against a global cabal responsible for corruption, child trafficking, and unspeakable acts. Q often hinted that they were operating at the highest levels of government, possibly within the Trump administration or the military, which only added to the intrigue. The choice to remain anonymous wasn't just a matter of practicality—it imbued Q with a mystique that kept followers engaged and guessing. Followers were left to speculate endlessly: Was Q a member of Trump's inner circle? A high-ranking intelligence officer? Or even Trump himself?

Q's posts, known as "Q drops," were written in a way that encouraged this kind of speculation. Each drop was a cryptic combination of questions, phrases, and military-style language. For example, instead of outright making a statement, Q would post something along the lines of, "The world is not as it seems. Who controls the media? Follow the money. Think. Q." This vague, puzzle-like language left room for interpretation, allowing followers to insert their own meanings and theories. The ambiguity made Q seem omniscient, as if they were leaving bread crumbs that only the most dedicated followers could understand. Unlike typical social media influencers, Q's power came from being unknown, yet always just within reach, as if they were someone close by, watching and guiding those who were "in the know."

The anonymous nature of Q was key to building a sense of trust within the QAnon community. It allowed followers to project their own beliefs, frustrations, and hopes onto this mysterious figure. Q's identity remained an open question, a riddle that added to the movement's allure. This uncertainty made Q seem both everywhere and nowhere, like a voice from within the establishment reaching out to those on the outside. Q's anonymity became part of the message, symbolizing a whistleblower forced into secrecy due to the overwhelming power of the cabal they were allegedly working against. In a time of growing distrust toward government institutions and the media, Q's supposed insider status gave the movement an air of legitimacy. Many saw Q as a courageous patriot risking everything to share the truth.

Early Q drops painted a vivid picture of Trump as a "savior" fighting this powerful cabal from within the White House. The posts described Trump's presidency as part of a larger plan to dismantle this corrupt network, promising followers that "The Storm"—a day of mass arrests and justice—was coming. Q reassured followers that Trump was not acting alone; he was supported by a coalition of loyal military generals and intelligence agents, all working behind the scenes to restore justice. To QAnon believers, this narrative explained why Trump's presidency often seemed chaotic or unconventional: it was all part of the plan, and the apparent disorder was a smokescreen hiding a grand strategy. This framing elevated Trump from a political figure to a hero, a man fulfilling a destiny that only the "awake" could see.

While Q remained hidden behind their cryptic posts, their use of military-style language and jargon led followers to believe that they were not only a government insider but also someone with a deep understanding of military operations. Terms like "The Storm" and "Great Awakening" gave the impression of a larger, coordinated effort—an invisible battle happening out of sight but poised to erupt at any moment. This approach wasn't just about adding drama; it created a shared language and identity for QAnon followers, making them feel as if they were part of an elite group with exclusive access to hidden knowledge. The idea of being among the chosen few who understood the real workings of the world fed into a sense of superiority, adding a sense of purpose to their lives.

The question of Q's identity became a crucial part of QAnon's mythology. The fact that followers didn't know who Q was actually strengthened their loyalty. Unlike a public figure who might be questioned or criticized, Q's faceless nature made them immune to personal attacks, creating an air of untouchable authority. Moreover, it allowed followers to believe that Q could be anyone—perhaps even someone they knew. This anonymity created a compelling and tantalizing mystery, fueling endless online speculation and discussions. Some followers developed theories that Q was former National Security Advisor Michael Flynn or White House aide Dan Scavino. Others went so far as to believe that Q was Trump himself, using the persona to communicate directly with his supporters. This speculation only added to the community's engagement, creating a sense of shared mission as they searched for clues and decoded the identity of their leader.

Q's anonymity became a powerful tool, not just in building intrigue but in fostering a sense of community and loyalty. Followers saw themselves as part of a secret resistance, working alongside an anonymous patriot to expose corruption and bring justice. For those who believed, Q wasn't just a messenger but a symbol of defiance, a beacon of truth shining in a world of lies. In time, Q's identity would become less important than the movement itself, but in those early days, the mystery of Q—the anonymous insider—was the spark that ignited a conspiracy theory unlike anything the world had seen before.

3. The "Great Awakening": Echoes of Past Conspiracy Theories

The QAnon conspiracy wasn't born in a vacuum. It drew heavily on a tangled web of earlier conspiracies, moral panics, and age-old fears that had simmered in Western culture for centuries. Central to QAnon's mythos was the idea of a "Great Awakening," an impending moment when the truth about a global cabal would be revealed, and the public would "wake up" to the reality of elite corruption, child trafficking, and Satanic rituals. For QAnon followers, this awakening was not just a revelation but a redemptive moment—a promise that, in the end, good would triumph over evil.

This theme of a hidden, malevolent force pulling the strings from the shadows is a familiar one. From the anti-Semitic fabrication *The Protocols of the Elders of Zion* to the paranoia of the Illuminati, history is filled with conspiracy theories claiming that a small, secretive group is controlling global events. Each new iteration adapts these themes to fit the anxieties of its time. In the early 20th century, The Protocols presented Jews as orchestrators of a plot to control world governments, feeding into the prejudice that contributed to the horrors of the Holocaust. The Illuminati, another popular conspiracy theory, painted the image of a clandestine group working behind the scenes to create a "New World Order," manipulating world events to gain ultimate control. QAnon, whether consciously or not, revived these ideas, channeling a fear of hidden elites into its core narrative.

The "Great Awakening" offered an answer to the age-old question posed by conspiracy theories: Why do bad things happen? Rather than accepting the complex interplay of political, economic, and social forces, QAnon presented a clear and emotionally satisfying answer: evil elites were at fault, and a reckoning was coming.

This framing aligned with centuries of "awakening" narratives, especially religious ones, that promised enlightenment and liberation from corrupt forces. For QAnon believers, this "awakening" mirrored the Christian idea of revelation or redemption, appealing to those seeking a clear battle between good and evil.

But QAnon didn't stop with vague accusations of elite corruption; it embraced one of the most disturbing moral panics in recent American history—the Satanic Panic of the 1980s. During that era, a wave of fear spread across the United States as accusations of Satanic ritual abuse surfaced in daycare centers and schools. Stories emerged of hidden networks engaging in ritualistic abuse of children, sparking a media frenzy and numerous criminal trials, most of which were later proven to be baseless. Yet, the fear of Satan-worshipping pedophiles took hold, causing mass hysteria and shaping American anxieties about children's safety and moral decay.

QAnon echoed these anxieties almost point for point. In Q's narrative, members of the cabal were not just criminals; they were Satan-worshipping pedophiles conducting ritualistic abuses on children. This twist transformed political opponents into something far more sinister than corrupt bureaucrats or out-of-touch elites—it made them monsters, beings capable of the worst imaginable evils. The language QAnon used—references to adrenochrome harvesting and child trafficking—drew directly from the Satanic Panic's accusations, repackaging them for a modern audience. In doing so, QAnon tapped into deeply embedded fears, creating an us-versus-them mentality that justified its extreme accusations.

The "Great Awakening" also absorbed aspects of anti-establishment conspiracies that had been brewing for decades, particularly in the wake of events like Watergate, the Vietnam War, and 9/11. Each of these moments deepened public distrust in government institutions and the media, laying the groundwork for a worldview that saw hidden agendas in every corner of society. By the time QAnon emerged in 2017, there was already a widespread sense of disenfranchisement and disillusionment, especially among certain segments of the American population. QAnon's narrative played into this, suggesting that mainstream media and government institutions were not just biased but actively participating in a plot to enslave humanity. In this narrative, Trump and Q were the only sources of "real" information, and traditional news outlets became "fake news," mouthpieces of the cabal.

To QAnon followers, the "Great Awakening" represented a personal journey as much as a collective one. Becoming "awake" meant rejecting the mainstream narratives presented by the media, academia, and government, and embracing an alternative reality where hidden truths could be found only by those willing to dig deeply enough. Q's messages encouraged this process, often urging followers to "do your own research" and "think for yourself." This call to independent thinking resonated with people who felt alienated by mainstream culture and empowered them to believe they were privy to a higher truth. For many, this sense of awakening was exhilarating, a feeling of finally seeing beyond the illusions they believed were fed to the public.

QAnon's "Great Awakening" wasn't just about revealing a secret cabal; it was about self-empowerment and belonging. It transformed its followers into members of a "chosen" group, a community that saw through the lies and manipulations of the elites. This feeling of special knowledge and moral superiority created a strong bond among QAnon adherents. Online groups, forums, and message boards became virtual congregations, places where followers shared their revelations, supported one another, and spread the message to others who were "still asleep." They saw themselves as modern-day truth seekers, warriors for justice standing against the forces of darkness.

The "Great Awakening" gave QAnon a powerful sense of purpose, rooted in historical fears and amplified by contemporary distrust and disillusionment. It promised its followers not only an answer to their questions and anxieties but also a path toward a heroic destiny. To believers, the "awakening" was more than a revelation; it was a call to arms. QAnon had done more than revive old conspiracies—it had given them new life and, for its followers, a purpose.

4. The Role of Disillusionment in the U.S. Political Climate

The rise of QAnon cannot be understood without recognizing the deep-seated disillusionment that had taken root in the United States, particularly in the years leading up to its emergence. Disillusionment with the political system, economic despair, and a widespread erosion of trust in traditional institutions created fertile ground for a theory as all-encompassing as QAnon to flourish. QAnon offered a simple, if shocking, explanation for the complex issues facing society: the world's problems were not the result of human fallibility or systemic failure, but rather the calculated evil of a hidden cabal. This narrative resonated strongly in an environment where people felt left behind, unheard, and betrayed.

By 2017, the United States was more politically polarized than it had been in decades. The 2016 presidential election had driven a wedge through American society, exposing cultural, economic, and ideological divides that had long simmered under the surface. Donald Trump's rise to power capitalized on this division, as he presented himself as an outsider, a man willing to take on what he called the "swamp" in Washington, D.C. His campaign resonated with voters who felt abandoned by the political establishment and disillusioned with both parties, particularly in rural areas and regions hit hardest by deindustrialization. Trump's victory fueled a new wave of populism, and for many of his supporters, he symbolized a last chance to restore what they felt had been lost. But this hope was tempered by an increasing paranoia that the "deep state"—a term used to describe an alleged hidden network of elites embedded within the government—was working to undermine Trump's efforts and maintain its stranglehold on power.

This "deep state" concept is central to QAnon's narrative. It allowed followers to rationalize the challenges and setbacks Trump faced in office as the work of unseen, nefarious forces. Every policy blocked, every investigation launched, and every critique from the media became evidence of the deep state's opposition to Trump and, by extension, to "the people." The idea that an entrenched group of elites within the government was actively working against the president fueled a growing sense of distrust, not only toward individual politicians but toward the entire political system. QAnon tapped into this distrust, offering its followers a narrative in which Trump was waging a heroic battle against these dark forces, fighting to dismantle a corrupt system that had betrayed the American people.

Beyond politics, there was also a sense of economic disillusionment that added to QAnon's appeal. In the years after the Great Recession of 2008, many Americans had not recovered financially, even as the stock market soared and corporate profits reached new heights. Wealth inequality grew increasingly visible, with a small percentage of Americans accumulating unprecedented wealth while working- and middle-class families struggled to make ends meet. This disparity contributed to a feeling that the "American Dream" was slipping away and that traditional avenues of social mobility were closing off. For those hit hardest, it was not a leap to believe that the system was rigged—that unseen forces were working to keep wealth and power concentrated in the hands of a few, at the expense of ordinary people.

In this climate of economic frustration, QAnon's accusations of a global cabal controlling wealth and power struck a chord. The theory promised not only an explanation but also a scapegoat for followers' struggles. Rather than blaming complex economic policies or global trends, QAnon directed frustration toward a group of elites that supposedly controlled the system from behind the scenes. The idea that these elites were involved in morally reprehensible activities, like child trafficking, intensified the anger and made the stakes feel even higher. QAnon offered its followers a clear-cut villain, giving a name and face to the forces they felt were holding them back. The theory painted a picture of a rigged world where suffering wasn't a byproduct of broken systems but the calculated work of evil individuals.

Another key factor in this disillusionment was the erosion of trust in traditional media. The years leading up to QAnon's rise were marked by growing skepticism toward mainstream news sources, exacerbated by the widespread cry of "fake news" that became a hallmark of Trump's presidency. His administration repeatedly questioned the legitimacy of media outlets, portraying them as biased, corrupt, and aligned with the so-called deep state. This skepticism was reinforced by both real instances of media misreporting and the intense partisanship that characterized American media. Many Americans, feeling increasingly isolated from what they saw as a coastal media elite, turned away from traditional news sources in search of alternative information. This rejection of mainstream media created a fertile environment for conspiracy theories to take root, as people sought explanations that aligned with their existing suspicions and fears.

QAnon provided an appealing alternative to traditional news. The "Q drops" and the movement's online communities allowed followers to "do their own research," a phrase that became almost a mantra within the movement. For followers, this independent research felt empowering, giving them a sense of control over their understanding of world events. Rather than passively consuming media, they were piecing together clues, decoding messages, and building their own narrative. In doing so, QAnon followers could see themselves as truth-seekers uncovering hidden realities, in stark contrast to a public they viewed as "asleep" and unaware of the dark forces shaping the world.

This shift to "independent research" was especially appealing in a time of institutional mistrust, as it allowed QAnon adherents to become active participants in the story, reinforcing their belief in Q's revelations. This sense of participation offered a unique allure that traditional media could not provide. Rather than merely observing the news, QAnon followers felt they were engaged in a larger battle for truth, actively working to expose the evil that mainstream sources supposedly refused to acknowledge. The power of this participatory experience gave followers a renewed sense of purpose, a chance to be part of something larger than themselves, and a community to belong to.

Together, these factors—political polarization, economic frustration, and distrust of traditional media—created a perfect storm for QAnon's rise. QAnon was able to channel deep-seated frustrations and anxieties, offering its followers not only a way to make sense of a world that felt increasingly hostile but also a path to take action. In an age where people felt powerless and betrayed, QAnon offered hope in the form of a narrative that promised justice, vindication, and a brighter future for those "awake" enough to see the truth.

5. The Digital Soldiers: Early Followers and Their Role

From the very beginning, QAnon was more than just a conspiracy theory—it was a call to action. Q's cryptic posts encouraged followers not only to believe but to actively participate in what they saw as a struggle between good and evil. This invitation to become "digital soldiers" transformed passive readers into engaged participants, building a sense of community and purpose among followers. Early adopters, often referred to within the movement as "anons," became instrumental in spreading and interpreting Q's messages, creating the foundation for a movement that would expand far beyond the dark corners of the internet.

The concept of the digital soldier began with Q's insistence that followers "do their own research" rather than trusting mainstream narratives. For many followers, this message was empowering; it offered them a role in what they believed to be a covert operation to expose corruption and dismantle an evil cabal. Q drops were often presented as puzzles or coded messages that required careful analysis to decipher. Followers eagerly took up the task, poring over every word, timestamp, and symbol to uncover hidden meanings. This approach turned QAnon into a kind of interactive mystery game, where each Q drop was a new clue to be solved. It made followers feel as though they were piecing together a grand puzzle and uncovering secrets that the general public could not see.

The process of decoding Q drops and spreading information became a community-driven effort, with followers creating online hubs on platforms like Reddit, 8chan, and later, Facebook and Twitter. Within these communities, QAnon adherents would collaborate on "baking" Q's messages, a process of analyzing, interpreting, and debating each post's meaning to produce a coherent narrative. This practice of group analysis fostered a strong sense of camaraderie. Followers were no longer isolated individuals with fringe beliefs; they were part of a collective engaged in a shared mission. These online spaces acted as echo chambers, where Q's vague and open-ended messages could be interpreted in ways that reinforced followers' beliefs, creating a self-sustaining cycle of validation and reinforcement.

Digital soldiers saw themselves as guardians of the truth, responsible for spreading their findings to those who were still "asleep." Q's call to "Wake up!" became a rallying cry, and followers took on the task of awakening friends, family members, and even strangers. They shared QAnon content across social media, produced YouTube videos, created memes, and organized online campaigns to promote Q's message. The movement's presence grew rapidly as digital soldiers spread their message far beyond Q's original posts. Memes, in particular, became a powerful tool; they distilled complex theories into easily shareable visuals and phrases, allowing QAnon to reach a much wider audience. Memes became both a recruiting tool and a badge of identity within the movement, marking followers as members of an "in-group" that understood the hidden truths.

As the movement gained traction, certain followers rose to prominence as influencers within the QAnon community. These influencers, often charismatic figures skilled at interpreting Q drops, became trusted voices, guiding other followers and reinforcing key messages. They produced video breakdowns, ran QAnon-centric social media pages, and sometimes even claimed to have additional insider knowledge. Figures like these served as intermediaries between Q and the broader community, shaping the direction of QAnon interpretations and adding layers of meaning to Q's often cryptic messages. Some of these influencers turned their roles into careers, generating revenue through donations, merchandise, and paid memberships, which incentivized them to keep followers engaged and invested. They became not just amplifiers of QAnon's message but also gatekeepers, steering the movement in ways that kept followers both informed and fiercely loyal.

As digital soldiers worked to spread the message, QAnon's reach grew beyond the internet, spilling into real-world events. Followers organized rallies, attended Trump's political events, and proudly displayed QAnon merchandise. The movement's visibility increased, especially as some QAnon symbols and slogans began appearing at Trump rallies. "Where We Go One, We Go All" (WWG1WGA), a phrase popularized by Q, became a rallying cry for followers and even a symbol of loyalty to the cause. Through these real-world expressions, QAnon transitioned from an online community to a visible social movement, attracting the attention of mainstream media and public figures. This visibility reinforced the digital soldiers' sense of importance and impact, further fueling their commitment to the cause.

This process of participation and public display fostered a deep sense of purpose and belonging among QAnon followers. For many digital soldiers, QAnon became more than a theory; it was a worldview that gave them direction and a mission. They believed they were part of a historic moment, a "Great Awakening" that would reshape society and reveal hidden truths. This sense of mission transformed ordinary individuals into activists who saw their work as essential to a righteous cause. For some, QAnon provided a sense of identity that they felt was lacking in their personal lives—a way to feel significant and part of something larger than themselves.

In many ways, the digital soldier phenomenon was the heart of QAnon's success. By turning followers into participants, Q had crafted a movement that was self-sustaining and constantly growing. Followers weren't just consuming information; they were actively shaping, interpreting, and spreading it. This participatory nature made QAnon feel like a living, evolving entity, something that could adapt and grow with each new Q drop. Digital soldiers didn't just follow Q; they embodied the movement, each becoming a beacon of its message and a warrior in its cause. For QAnon adherents, this wasn't just a conspiracy theory—it was a movement, a mission, and, for many, a profound sense of purpose.

Chapter 2: The Central Myth: The Cabal

1. Defining the Cabal: Who Are the Elites?

Central to QAnon's theory is the concept of a powerful "cabal," a shadowy collective of elites who supposedly control the world from behind the scenes. This cabal is not just any group of influential people; it is an alliance of the most powerful figures across politics, entertainment, finance, and business, united by sinister motives and secret rituals. To QAnon followers, these elites aren't merely wealthy and privileged—they are part of a coordinated and highly secretive network with an agenda that transcends borders and industries. This shadow government, or "deep state," is believed to operate independently of elected governments, working in the interests of a global elite while orchestrating world events to maintain their power and wealth.

The concept of the cabal draws directly from a longstanding human tendency to distrust those in power, particularly when they are perceived as remote or inaccessible. Within QAnon's framework, prominent figures like the Clintons, George Soros, and Bill Gates are commonly portrayed as central figures in the cabal, depicted as individuals with outsized influence who operate without accountability.

Hollywood celebrities are also cast as pawns or active members of the cabal, seen as both manipulators of public opinion and participants in morally corrupt activities. Figures like Tom Hanks, Oprah Winfrey, and Ellen DeGeneres are frequent targets of QAnon's accusations, their fame and wealth recast as evidence of hidden alliances and disturbing secrets. These individuals, once celebrated for their success and influence, are viewed as sinister figures by QAnon adherents, operating not for public good but for self-serving, malevolent purposes.

At the center of this supposed cabal is a unique combination of political and financial elites. QAnon posits that leading figures within the Democratic Party and high-profile corporate executives work together to manipulate government policies, economies, and social narratives, promoting their hidden agenda. According to QAnon, these elites use their influence to control major institutions and keep the masses distracted or misinformed, whether through the mainstream media, global organizations like the United Nations and the World Health Organization, or massive social media platforms. This view builds on the popular distrust in centralized institutions, painting these powerful bodies as extensions of the cabal's agenda rather than neutral organizations serving the public good.

The cabal's supposed membership and activities play into a narrative that the QAnon community perceives as a black-and-white moral dichotomy. Those inside the cabal are portrayed as morally depraved, their wealth and influence resulting from ruthless exploitation and sinister schemes. This portrayal allows followers to interpret world events in terms of good versus evil, with little room for nuance. Individuals seen as opposed to the cabal—such as Donald Trump—are cast as heroic figures waging a noble battle against these elites. Trump's opposition to the establishment is viewed not as typical political resistance but as evidence of his role as an "outsider" who is genuinely working for the people, unlike the supposedly corrupt figures that populate the cabal.

This narrative draws on familiar archetypes. The idea of a select group of wealthy elites pulling the strings of global events has echoes in conspiracy theories dating back centuries, including the anti-Semitic conspiracy theories surrounding the Rothschilds and the Illuminati. These older narratives are reframed within QAnon to fit modern fears about globalism, digital surveillance, and mass media manipulation. By connecting present-day elites to historical narratives of secret societies and hidden power structures, QAnon creates an all-encompassing worldview where the cabal is responsible for nearly every significant social, political, or economic issue.

To followers, the belief in a hidden cabal provides a straightforward answer to the often overwhelming complexities of modern life. Rather than wrestling with the intricacies of global politics, economic inequality, or social justice, they find it easier to believe that a shadowy network of elites is orchestrating world events for its own benefit. This belief allows them to simplify a chaotic world into a narrative that aligns with their values and concerns, casting the elites as villains and themselves as enlightened truth-seekers fighting back. For many, this narrative offers a sense of clarity and purpose in a world that can otherwise seem hostile and incomprehensible.

In QAnon's world, the cabal isn't just a group of influential people; it is the manifestation of all societal evils, a pervasive force that must be fought at all costs. This perception makes the concept of the cabal central to QAnon's ideology. By framing specific elites as members of a morally corrupt, all-powerful group, QAnon gives its followers a clear, identifiable target for their frustration and anger—a "villain" they can unite against, fueling the movement's growth and commitment. The cabal, in essence, becomes the embodiment of everything followers feel is wrong with society, making it the foundational myth on which QAnon builds its narrative of "good versus evil."

2. The Accusations: Child Trafficking and Ritualistic Abuse

At the core of QAnon's mythology are disturbing allegations that the cabal engages in child trafficking, pedophilia, and Satanic rituals to maintain power and wealth. These accusations aren't presented as fringe beliefs within the movement; they are fundamental tenets, providing a moral justification for the fight followers believe they are waging. By framing the elites as perpetrators of such horrific acts, QAnon creates a clear, emotionally charged enemy that followers feel compelled to oppose. This dark narrative taps into universal fears about children's safety and innocence, using these fears to evoke a visceral reaction that galvanizes QAnon's base.

The belief that the cabal engages in child trafficking is rooted in a combination of historical moral panics and modern anxieties. The idea of Satan-worshipping elites conducting ritualistic abuse is not new; it echoes the Satanic Panic of the 1980s, a period when fear of Satanic cults abusing children swept across America. During the Satanic Panic, numerous accusations surfaced, often leading to legal trials and public hysteria, but almost all of these allegations were later debunked. Yet, the fear remained deeply embedded in American consciousness, and QAnon resurrected it, adapting it to the contemporary context. In the QAnon narrative, the cabal is not only politically corrupt but also morally depraved, a group of people so twisted that they commit unspeakable acts against society's most vulnerable.

QAnon goes further by alleging that members of the cabal harvest "adrenochrome" from the blood of children, which they supposedly use as a form of drug or elixir to maintain youth and vitality. This macabre detail has its roots in both horror fiction and conspiracy lore, where adrenochrome has been a recurring theme. Within QAnon's mythology, adrenochrome is not merely a substance but a symbol of the cabal's insatiable greed and disregard for humanity. The adrenochrome narrative adds a layer of horror to the cabal's alleged activities, reinforcing the idea that they are not just immoral but inhuman. This belief places the cabal in a realm of monstrosity that defies typical understandings of evil, making it easy for followers to view them as irredeemable and worthy of the harshest punishment.

The emotional appeal of these allegations cannot be overstated. Child trafficking and abuse are universally condemned, and QAnon capitalizes on this near-universal moral consensus to drive a wedge between "good" and "evil" as defined by the movement. Followers who might otherwise be skeptical of conspiracy theories find themselves drawn in by the need to protect children and oppose those who would harm them. This appeal is especially powerful because it allows followers to see themselves as heroes on a noble mission. In their eyes, they are not just exposing political corruption but rescuing innocent children from unimaginable horrors, an act that justifies any means necessary to achieve their goals.

What makes these allegations so potent is their ability to bypass rational debate and appeal directly to emotions. By framing the cabal's actions in terms of child abuse and Satanic rituals, QAnon eliminates the possibility of nuance or compromise. Anyone who questions or opposes QAnon's beliefs can be cast as an enabler or sympathizer of the cabal. This all-or-nothing mindset fosters an "us versus them" mentality, encouraging followers to see the world in stark moral terms. The movement creates a sense of urgency around the idea that children are being harmed on a massive scale, making it morally imperative for followers to act and spread QAnon's message.

These accusations are further amplified through social media, where graphic, heart-wrenching images and stories related to child trafficking are circulated widely. QAnon followers often share content about missing children or child abuse cases unrelated to the movement as "evidence" of the cabal's activities. The movement has co-opted hashtags like #SaveTheChildren, blending genuine concern for child safety with baseless conspiracies about the cabal. This tactic blurs the line between reality and fiction, making it difficult for outside observers to distinguish legitimate activism from QAnon's conspiratorial agenda. By doing this, QAnon taps into real-world fears and harnesses them to promote its core beliefs, drawing in followers who might not otherwise engage with conspiracy theories.

The emotional weight of these accusations transforms QAnon from a conspiracy theory into what followers see as a moral crusade. To them, this is not simply a battle over political power or social control—it is a fight for the safety and future of children everywhere. By positioning themselves as protectors of children, followers adopt a sense of righteousness that justifies their belief in QAnon and strengthens their loyalty to the movement. This unwavering moral conviction is one of QAnon's most powerful tools, making it exceptionally difficult for followers to disengage or question the movement's validity.

In sum, QAnon's accusations of child trafficking, pedophilia, and ritualistic abuse are foundational to its mythology, imbuing the movement with a sense of moral urgency that keeps followers engaged and loyal. These claims are designed not just to explain the world's problems but to present the cabal as an existential threat to society, one that must be eradicated. For followers, fighting the cabal is a moral duty, making it easy for them to dismiss any opposition as morally compromised. This framing not only defines the cabal as irredeemably evil but also makes followers feel morally superior and obligated to spread QAnon's message. Through these disturbing and powerful accusations, QAnon sustains its followers' commitment and transforms a conspiracy theory into a personal crusade.

3. The Cabal's Control Over Global Systems

In QAnon's worldview, the cabal doesn't merely exist in secret—it actively controls society's most critical institutions. Followers believe that this elite network extends its influence over governments, the media, financial systems, and even global organizations, manipulating events to maintain its power and serve its sinister agenda. This aspect of the theory draws from classic "puppet master" conspiracies, framing the cabal as a hidden hand that shapes every aspect of life. To QAnon adherents, the cabal is an all-powerful entity capable of orchestrating everything from financial crises to wars, bending entire nations to its will in a bid to keep the masses distracted and under control.

One of QAnon's primary claims is that the cabal has infiltrated the highest levels of government. According to the theory, prominent political figures, particularly within the Democratic Party, are merely puppets controlled by the cabal. QAnon frames these individuals as agents of a hidden agenda, willing to sell out their countries for personal gain and cabal loyalty. Figures like Hillary Clinton, Barack Obama, and Nancy Pelosi are frequently portrayed as key members of this network, wielding influence not for public service but to advance the cabal's interests. This view allows followers to dismiss political decisions and policies they disagree with as part of a grander conspiracy, rather than as differing ideologies or policy perspectives. To them, the government is not a democratic institution but a corrupted structure that serves only the cabal's objectives.

In addition to government influence, QAnon posits that the cabal controls the media, framing it as a propaganda machine used to manipulate public perception and suppress the truth. This belief plays into a common distrust of mainstream media, which many Americans see as biased or sensationalistic. QAnon takes this skepticism further, claiming that news outlets, journalists, and even Hollywood celebrities are pawns of the cabal, used to keep the public uninformed and docile. To QAnon followers, stories that don't fit their worldview are seen as "fake news" and evidence of the cabal's reach. This perception allows followers to reject anything critical of QAnon as part of a larger cover-up, creating an echo chamber where only "approved" information aligns with their beliefs.

The cabal's supposed reach extends beyond national borders, infiltrating global organizations such as the United Nations, the World Health Organization, and the International Monetary Fund. In QAnon's view, these institutions are not dedicated to international cooperation but serve as tools for the cabal to exert influence on a global scale. Followers interpret initiatives like climate change regulations, public health mandates, and international trade agreements as cabal tactics to consolidate power and control. For example, efforts to combat climate change are often framed as a way for the cabal to impose restrictions and regulations that benefit their interests at the expense of ordinary people. This distrust is particularly powerful because it allows followers to see global issues as manufactured crises designed to keep the public fearful and compliant.

Financial systems are another focal point of QAnon's narrative. The cabal is seen as manipulating global markets and economies, engineering recessions and financial collapses to tighten its grip on wealth and power. This belief taps into widespread discontent about economic inequality and distrust in big banks and financial institutions. QAnon followers see economic hardship not as the result of complex global forces but as a deliberate strategy by the cabal to create a world where they hold all the wealth and power while ordinary people struggle. By blaming financial systems on a hidden cabal, QAnon provides a simple answer to questions about wealth disparity, offering followers a clear villain to hold responsible for their economic challenges.

QAnon's claims about the cabal's control over these institutions echo older conspiracy theories about a "New World Order" or the Illuminati—secret societies allegedly controlling global affairs for centuries. By drawing on these established conspiracy narratives, QAnon taps into deeply embedded fears about losing sovereignty, privacy, and freedom. The theory gives followers a clear explanation for why so many aspects of modern life feel beyond their control: it isn't the result of natural evolution or unintended consequences but the deliberate manipulation of a cabal that is omnipotent and malevolent.

Belief in the cabal's reach creates a pervasive sense of powerlessness among QAnon followers, reinforcing the need for a savior figure like Trump, whom they believe is working to dismantle these corrupt systems from within. It fosters a world where ordinary people feel helpless in the face of a vast and invisible enemy but empowered through their allegiance to QAnon. Followers see themselves as "awake," capable of recognizing the cabal's machinations, while the rest of society remains "asleep" and oblivious to the sinister forces at work.

By framing the cabal as controlling all major institutions, QAnon provides a worldview in which every crisis, scandal, or disagreement is not just a result of chance or conflict but an intentional act by the cabal to manipulate society. This worldview creates a powerful "us versus them" mentality that keeps followers engaged and distrustful of any information or authority that doesn't align with QAnon's message. The cabal's alleged control over global systems becomes the ultimate justification for the movement's beliefs and actions, solidifying its followers' commitment to "fighting back" in whatever ways they can.

In QAnon's framework, the cabal is omnipresent, its reach touching every corner of society. This narrative doesn't just simplify complex social and economic problems; it weaponizes them, turning them into evidence of an all-powerful enemy lurking in the shadows. By casting the cabal as a dark force orchestrating global events, QAnon offers followers a lens through which they can interpret the world—a lens that, to them, makes everything finally make sense.

4. Debunking the Myths: Evidence and Counterarguments

Despite its complex mythology and detailed claims, QAnon's central narrative about a secretive, all-powerful cabal collapses under scrutiny. In reality, the evidence supporting QAnon's accusations is either nonexistent, wildly misinterpreted, or deliberately fabricated. Investigative journalists, law enforcement, and researchers have consistently debunked the theory, highlighting how QAnon's "proof" often relies on unverified sources, selective interpretation, and misleading information. Yet, the lack of credible evidence has not weakened the movement's popularity among its followers, who tend to interpret contradictory information as part of a broader cover-up, reinforcing their commitment rather than diminishing it.

One of the key tactics QAnon uses to support its narrative is the misinterpretation of legitimate news stories, often taking real-world events or quotes out of context to fit the theory's agenda. For instance, publicized incidents involving child trafficking are often co-opted as "proof" of the cabal's existence, even when these cases are unrelated to any organized conspiracy. A notable example is the way QAnon has latched onto legitimate anti-trafficking organizations and high-profile cases, repurposing them to reinforce its own narrative. Although the cases QAnon cites are real and deeply troubling, they have no connection to the alleged global cabal. This selective use of information distorts genuine efforts to combat trafficking and shifts focus away from actual offenders, casting a cloud of misinformation over a serious issue.

QAnon also uses fabricated stories to bolster its claims, frequently sharing baseless rumors and doctored images on social media as evidence of the cabal's influence. False claims about high-profile arrests, hidden indictments, and covert military operations are common, despite a complete lack of corroborating evidence. For example, followers often circulate rumors of celebrities or politicians being secretly detained, facing trial, or executed, with "doubles" or "clones" allegedly standing in for public appearances. These claims persist even when the individuals in question appear in public or provide real-time evidence of their whereabouts. Rather than prompting followers to question the validity of the theory, these inconsistencies are often rationalized within the movement as further proof of the cabal's reach—another layer of deception to maintain control over the narrative.

Investigative journalists have played a critical role in debunking QAnon's assertions, often tracing the origins of these rumors to anonymous social media accounts or online forums where disinformation thrives. Fact-checking organizations have systematically debunked hundreds of QAnon claims, often providing clear, evidence-based refutations. Reports from reputable outlets, for example, have examined and disproven QAnon's allegations of child trafficking networks tied to high-profile figures, finding no verifiable connection. Yet, QAnon followers often dismiss mainstream journalism as part of the cabal's disinformation network, making fact-checking efforts less effective within the movement itself. The refusal to accept external verification is a cornerstone of the conspiracy, as it allows followers to remain within a closed-loop belief system.

Law enforcement agencies, including the FBI, have also weighed in on QAnon, warning that the conspiracy poses a growing domestic threat due to its ability to incite violence and spread dangerous misinformation. The FBI has labeled QAnon and similar theories as potential sources of domestic terrorism, given the movement's tendency to promote vigilantism against perceived members of the cabal. The lack of evidence and credibility surrounding QAnon's accusations has not prevented followers from harassing, threatening, or even attempting to harm individuals they believe are part of the conspiracy. Numerous incidents of attempted or threatened violence have been tied to QAnon adherents, further highlighting the disconnect between the movement's beliefs and reality. These warnings from law enforcement are well-documented, yet QAnon followers often interpret such advisories as part of the supposed cover-up, proof that the cabal will go to any lengths to silence the "truth."

A critical examination of QAnon's core claims also reveals a reliance on logical fallacies and cognitive biases. Followers often engage in "confirmation bias," selectively gathering information that supports their beliefs while ignoring or rejecting anything that contradicts them. For instance, the use of vague, cryptic language in Q drops allows followers to find "hidden meanings" that align with their expectations. This phenomenon, known as "apophenia," is the tendency to perceive connections and patterns in unrelated information, a hallmark of conspiracy thinking. The process of interpreting Q drops often becomes a self-fulfilling prophecy, as followers project their anxieties and expectations onto the messages, turning ambiguity into confirmation. By relying on this interpretive process, QAnon builds a belief system that feels both personally validated and unassailable to its followers.

Despite the abundance of credible sources debunking QAnon's claims, many followers remain entrenched in the movement due to its psychological appeal. The conspiracy theory provides a sense of belonging, purpose, and certainty in a world that often feels confusing and disjointed. For some, acknowledging the movement's flaws would mean losing a core part of their identity, making it difficult to accept evidence that contradicts the cabal narrative. This attachment to QAnon is not based on logical arguments or factual evidence but on emotional investment. The theory provides answers to difficult questions and gives followers a framework through which they can view the world as ordered, understandable, and moral.

In sum, QAnon's accusations against the cabal have been debunked repeatedly through journalistic investigations, law enforcement reports, and logical analysis. Yet, the movement's adherents continue to interpret reality through the lens of conspiracy, turning every counterargument into further "proof" of the cabal's existence. By exploiting cognitive biases and emotional needs, QAnon has built a belief system that resists factual challenges, prioritizing narrative consistency over truth. For followers, the myth of the cabal is not simply a theory to be disproven but a worldview that offers clarity, purpose, and a sense of mission.

5. The Cabal as a Modern Moral Panic

The idea of a hidden, morally depraved cabal orchestrating evil from the shadows isn't a new phenomenon; it's the latest iteration of a recurring cultural theme known as a moral panic. Throughout history, societies have experienced waves of hysteria around perceived threats, often directed at marginalized or misunderstood groups. From the witch hunts of the 17th century to the Satanic Panic of the 1980s, these episodes of fear and outrage reflect society's deep-seated anxieties about corruption, vulnerability, and loss of control. QAnon's cabal narrative taps directly into these fears, framing elites as irredeemable villains whose actions threaten the very fabric of society. In doing so, QAnon's beliefs reflect—and amplify—cultural anxieties about the future, the safety of children, and the integrity of traditional values.

The Satanic Panic of the 1980s is one of the clearest predecessors to QAnon's beliefs. During this period, widespread fears emerged around allegations of Satanic ritual abuse, particularly in daycare centers and schools across the United States. Parents and communities believed that secret cults were abusing children in horrific ways as part of Satanic rites. Despite extensive investigations, almost none of these allegations were substantiated, and many of the accused were later exonerated. Yet, the panic persisted, driven by media reports, flawed psychological evaluations, and public fear. The Satanic Panic leveraged one of society's most vulnerable points—children's safety—and weaponized it to create a sense of moral urgency, much like QAnon's accusations against the cabal today.

QAnon repackages these historical fears for a modern audience, infusing them with 21st-century anxieties about government corruption, media manipulation, and elite privilege. The cabal narrative doesn't just draw on a fear of Satanic practices; it merges these older anxieties with contemporary concerns about the unchecked power of global elites. In QAnon's version, the cabal is more than a religious cult; it is a sophisticated network of politicians, billionaires, and celebrities who maintain their power through an organized system of trafficking and exploitation. This framing serves a dual purpose: it not only revives familiar fears but also updates them, making them relevant to an era where traditional authority figures and institutions are increasingly mistrusted.

QAnon's portrayal of the cabal reflects broader concerns about the erosion of traditional social structures, from family dynamics to religious values. Many QAnon followers are drawn to the movement because it offers a way to make sense of societal shifts they find desta-bilizing, from changing cultural norms to economic inequality. By casting the cabal as a corrupting influence that seeks to undermine moral values and control the masses, QAnon offers followers an ex-planation for why society feels unfamiliar and threatening. This idea of moral decay, driven by elite forces, allows followers to identify and "other" a group that they see as responsible for their discomfort, cre-ating a scapegoat onto which they can project their fears and frustra-tions.

The emotional resonance of the cabal narrative, like any moral panic, lies in its appeal to primal fears—specifically, the vulnerability of children. Child safety is a nearly universal concern, and QAnon uses this issue as a rallying cry to fuel outrage and commitment within its ranks. By claiming that powerful elites are actively harm-ing children, QAnon invokes a strong, immediate sense of moral duty in its followers. This moral imperative enables QAnon to gain traction even among people who may not fully buy into the move-ment's more outlandish claims. The mantra of protecting children gives the movement a veneer of legitimacy and urgency, allowing it to masquerade as a form of grassroots activism rather than an un-founded conspiracy theory.

Beyond its impact on individual beliefs, the QAnon-driven moral panic has real-world consequences. As QAnon followers em-brace the narrative that children are under immediate threat from powerful elites, many have taken matters into their own hands, en-gaging in "vigilante" actions against alleged cabal members or harass-ing public figures accused of these crimes. Law enforcement agencies have reported incidents where QAnon followers have threatened or attempted violence against people they perceive to be part of the ca-bal. This phenomenon shows how moral panics can lead to danger-ous, reactionary behaviors as people feel justified in taking extreme actions to protect what they believe to be under assault. In this way, QAnon's moral panic poses not only a threat to those falsely accused but also undermines the very institutions—law enforcement, media, and the justice system—that exist to protect society.

The cabal narrative also warps the public's understanding of real issues, particularly around child trafficking and exploitation. QAnon's focus on a mythical, elite-driven trafficking network diverts attention and resources from actual cases of child abuse, which often occur in local communities and involve people known to the victims rather than an elaborate global network. By monopolizing the conversation around child safety, QAnon's followers inadvertently create a smokescreen that hampers genuine efforts to protect vulnerable populations. Child protection organizations have voiced concerns that QAnon's focus on unsubstantiated claims is undermining real-world activism and spreading misinformation that complicates legitimate anti-trafficking work.

As a moral panic, QAnon's cabal myth reflects both timeless fears and modern anxieties. It taps into a desire to restore moral order, combat perceived corruption, and protect innocent lives—all of which are powerful motivators. Yet, by focusing these fears on a fictional enemy, QAnon diverts energy and attention from addressing the genuine challenges facing society. In doing so, it sustains itself as a cultural force, feeding off the very real frustrations of people who feel left behind or betrayed by the world around them. This cycle of fear and accusation is self-perpetuating, allowing QAnon to remain resilient even as its claims are repeatedly debunked.

Ultimately, QAnon's cabal narrative serves as a mirror to society's deepest fears and frustrations, distilling complex issues into a simple story of good versus evil. While the movement's claims about an elite-run cabal are unfounded, the moral panic it has ignited is very real, revealing widespread distrust, disillusionment, and a longing for clarity in an increasingly complicated world. By framing itself as a crusade against an ultimate evil, QAnon provides its followers with both a sense of purpose and an explanation for societal change, ensuring that the myth of the cabal endures even in the face of overwhelming evidence to the contrary.

Chapter 3: Trump, the Savior

1. The Digital Birth: 4chan, 8chan, and Anonymous Message Boards

In late October 2017, a mysterious figure known only as "Q" began posting cryptic messages on the internet message board 4chan. 4chan had long been a hub for alternative communities, conspiracy theories, and internet subcultures, making it the perfect breeding ground for an idea as radical as QAnon. Q claimed to possess "Q-level" security clearance, a top-secret designation within the U.S. Department of Energy, implying access to highly classified government information. Over time, these posts, known as "Q drops," would grow into a sprawling conspiracy theory. These early Q drops set the stage for a narrative that framed the world's most powerful people as part of a secret cabal involved in morally reprehensible activities, positioning then-President Donald Trump as a savior figure waging a hidden war against these elites.

The anonymity of platforms like 4chan and its successor, 8chan, was a crucial part of QAnon's development. Unlike mainstream social media sites like Facebook or Twitter, 4chan allowed users to post without revealing their identity, creating an environment where anything could be said with little consequence. This anonymity allowed "Q" to make bold, unverified claims while maintaining an aura of mystery and authority. Anonymity also provided Q's followers with the freedom to interpret these cryptic messages without external scrutiny, creating a self-reinforcing echo chamber where doubts could be minimized and theories could flourish. Followers were encouraged to "follow the breadcrumbs" left by Q, piecing together a narrative that was part treasure hunt, part puzzle, and part digital revolution.

Q's posts were unlike typical internet content; they were deliberately vague and filled with military-style language, open-ended questions, and symbolic references that left much room for interpretation. A typical Q drop might read something like, "The storm is upon us. Trust the plan. Follow the money." These ambiguous phrases were designed to be puzzling, requiring followers to sift through and interpret the meaning themselves. This cryptic style turned Q's messages into a sort of interactive mystery, where followers could collaborate and analyze clues, creating theories and drawing connections. The process of interpreting Q drops became known as "decoding" or "baking," with followers considering themselves "anons" or "bakers" piecing together the ultimate truth. This gamified approach gave followers a sense of agency, as though they were participating in an unfolding plot.

As Q's following grew, many users migrated from 4chan to 8chan, a platform with even fewer restrictions. 8chan was known for its commitment to free speech and refusal to moderate content, allowing communities to flourish regardless of their views. This unrestricted environment enabled QAnon's community to spread and deepen its theories without interference. On 8chan, Q drops became more frequent, and the community around them grew more organized. Followers created threads to decode Q's latest posts, dissecting every detail and discussing implications. Each Q drop was treated like a critical piece of intelligence, sparking debates and theories that could sometimes span hundreds of posts. Here, QAnon evolved from a conspiracy theory into a full-fledged movement, united by shared goals, beliefs, and a commitment to expose what they saw as the dark truth of society.

The digital landscape was crucial to QAnon's success. Anonymous boards like 4chan and 8chan offered an ecosystem where radical ideas could grow and flourish, connecting individuals who might otherwise have remained isolated in their beliefs. These platforms gave followers a sense of community and identity, reinforcing the idea that they were part of an elite group with access to hidden knowledge. Being part of QAnon wasn't just about consuming information; it was about collaborating, contributing, and sharing discoveries within a group that saw itself as enlightened. This sense of belonging created a powerful loyalty to Q and the movement, as followers felt they were part of something larger than themselves—a historic fight against evil.

QAnon's origins on 4chan and 8chan also cultivated a specific online culture. Unlike traditional social media platforms, where identity and reputation play a role, these anonymous boards encouraged unfiltered discourse and raw expression. Followers who might have been hesitant to share controversial views elsewhere felt liberated on these platforms, contributing to an environment where extreme ideas were not only accepted but celebrated. Q's use of secrecy and ambiguity further amplified this culture, as followers rallied around a shared purpose, believing they were uncovering the truth in a world controlled by lies. The open-ended nature of Q's drops allowed them to be interpreted in countless ways, and because no single interpretation was "correct," the community was free to build an increasingly intricate web of theories.

Over time, QAnon's early adopters would play a crucial role in bringing the theory from the anonymity of 4chan and 8chan to mainstream platforms like Facebook, Twitter, and YouTube. These early followers, emboldened by their sense of purpose, began creating QAnon-related content, spreading its symbols, slogans, and ideas across the internet. The anonymity of 4chan and 8chan may have fostered the movement's birth, but social media brought it into the public eye, amplifying its message and recruiting new followers. Yet, the movement's foundational culture of secrecy, conspiracy, and anonymous collaboration remained central to its identity.

By tapping into the power of digital anonymity and community-driven investigation, QAnon was able to flourish in an online environment that allowed ideas to spread freely, unchecked by conventional standards of credibility. What started as a few cryptic posts from an anonymous figure grew into a sprawling movement with millions of followers worldwide. The culture fostered on 4chan and 8chan, combined with Q's vague, open-ended messaging, created a potent mix of mystery, agency, and community—a digital playground where the theory could take on a life of its own, one post at a time. For QAnon followers, the internet was more than a source of information; it was a battlefield where they believed they were fighting for the soul of society itself.

2. Who is "Q"? The Anonymous Insider

The identity of "Q" is perhaps the most captivating mystery within the QAnon movement. Unlike traditional conspiracy theories, which often have identifiable leaders or creators, QAnon's central figure remains shrouded in secrecy. By claiming to be an anonymous government insider with "Q-level" security clearance—a real classification in the U.S. Department of Energy used to access top-secret information related to nuclear intelligence—Q set themselves apart from typical internet personalities or conspiracy theorists. Q's supposed credentials lent an air of authority and credibility, sparking intrigue and speculation among followers. Who was this figure? And what motivated them to risk everything by revealing secrets from within the highest ranks of government?

Q's anonymity wasn't just incidental; it was essential to the movement's allure. In a time of widespread distrust in government, media, and corporations, Q's hidden identity fueled speculation and wonder. The mystery surrounding Q's identity allowed followers to project their own ideas onto this enigmatic figure. Was Q a high-ranking military official? A Trump administration insider? Or perhaps even Trump himself? Each of these possibilities was debated, dissected, and argued over in the forums, adding layers of intrigue that only served to strengthen followers' attachment to the movement. For many, the possibility that Q could be someone close to power—or power itself—made the movement feel profoundly significant, as if they were receiving direct communications from the very top.

The nature of Q's communications further intensified this sense of connection. Unlike conventional leaders who might issue direct orders or statements, Q operated through cryptic "drops" or messages, composed of fragmented sentences, questions, and ambiguous clues. This cryptic style was both intentional and effective. Rather than giving explicit instructions, Q would often leave bread crumbs, encouraging followers to "do your own research" or "think for yourself." This approach had a dual effect: it fostered a sense of agency among followers, as they took on the role of investigators, and it allowed them to interpret Q's messages in ways that confirmed their own beliefs. Every drop became a puzzle, and every follower a "digital soldier," tasked with decoding and spreading the message.

To further enhance the mystique, Q's posts often included military-style jargon and terms that implied access to high-level intelligence. References to "The Storm," "the deep state," and "The Great Awakening" painted a picture of a vast, clandestine operation unfolding behind the scenes, one that only the initiated could understand. The use of these terms had a powerful psychological effect on followers, making them feel as though they were privy to insider knowledge and that they alone had the "real" understanding of world events. Followers began to see Q's posts as more than mere words; they were glimpses into a hidden war where stakes were existential, and they were on the side of truth and justice.

The ambiguity surrounding Q's identity also insulated the movement from criticism. Without a single, identifiable leader to hold accountable, QAnon became difficult to debunk in traditional terms. Any inconsistencies in Q's messages could be rationalized, as followers believed that disinformation was sometimes necessary to throw enemies off track. This logic created a self-reinforcing system where followers could dismiss contradictions as part of the strategy, further obscuring Q's identity and intentions. The lack of a public persona for Q meant that there was no face to question, critique, or hold responsible, making it easier for followers to continue believing even when reality seemed to contradict the theory.

The question of Q's true identity became a central preoccupation within the movement, leading to countless theories and speculations. Some followers believed that Q was Michael Flynn, the former National Security Advisor, while others suggested it could be Steve Bannon, a former White House strategist known for his populist rhetoric. Another theory posited that Q was actually a group of people, a team of "white hats" in the intelligence community working behind the scenes to expose the cabal. The belief that Q might be more than one person added a layer of complexity, allowing followers to rationalize the inconsistencies in tone or style across different Q drops. The possibility of a "Q team" reinforced the idea that

QAnon was not just a theory but a coordinated operation involving patriots in the highest ranks of government.

Yet the most captivating theory of all was that Q was actually Donald Trump himself, communicating directly with his supporters under a veil of anonymity. This idea turned QAnon into something much more than a conspiracy theory; it became a direct connection to the highest office in the United States. For followers who believed this, Q's drops were presidential messages in disguise, and each cryptic phrase carried the weight of Trump's supposed insider knowledge and authority. This theory reinforced Trump's role within QAnon as a heroic figure, leading a clandestine battle against evil forces. The notion that Q could be Trump himself turned followers into participants in a hidden narrative, creating a bond of trust and loyalty between them and the president.

In the absence of a concrete identity, Q became whatever followers needed Q to be—a lone patriot, a team of insiders, a general, or even the president. This ambiguity, combined with the open-ended nature of Q's messages, allowed followers to maintain their own interpretations and adapt the theory as needed. By remaining faceless, Q became an almost mythical figure, a symbol of resistance and truth that transcended individual identity. For followers, Q was no longer just a person (or people) dropping clues on the internet; Q was a movement, a mission, and a shared sense of purpose. The mystery of Q's identity became one of QAnon's greatest strengths, binding its followers together in a shared journey to reveal the hidden truths that, they believed, would one day change the world.

3. The "Great Awakening": Echoes of Past Conspiracy Theories

Central to QAnon's mythology is the promise of a "Great Awakening"—a moment when the truth about the world's elite will be exposed, and the masses will finally see the corruption that has been hidden from them for so long. For followers, the Great Awakening isn't just a metaphor; it's a prophesied event that will transform society, bringing justice, vindication, and moral clarity. In QAnon's narrative, this awakening will culminate in a dramatic reckoning for members of the cabal—arrests, trials, and, in some interpretations, public executions. The promise of the Great Awakening gives followers a sense of hope and purpose, allowing them to feel that they are on the precipice of a historic turning point. This idea, however, is not unique to QAnon; it borrows from and echoes many past conspiracy theories and moral panics, each fueled by a similar vision of good versus evil, order versus chaos.

The concept of a secret, malevolent elite controlling the world has deep roots in Western history. One of the earliest and most notorious examples is *The Protocols of the Elders of Zion*, an anti-Semitic forgery published in the early 20th century that claimed to reveal a Jewish plot for global domination. Despite being debunked repeatedly, the Protocols spread widely, stoking fear, anger, and prejudice, and paving the way for numerous anti-Semitic conspiracies. Later, during the Cold War, anti-communist sentiments fueled fears of a "Red Scare," where ordinary Americans believed communists had infiltrated the government, Hollywood, and academia. These fears prompted waves of suspicion, blacklists, and public accusations, all rooted in the idea that a hidden enemy was working to undermine society from within. QAnon's Great Awakening draws on these historical narratives, reframing familiar fears for a modern audience and presenting elites as corrupt figures working against the public's best interests.

But QAnon's vision of the Great Awakening goes beyond political paranoia—it also evokes echoes of the Satanic Panic of the 1980s. During this period, widespread fears about Satanic ritual abuse took hold in the United States, with claims that hidden cults were sacrificing children and committing horrific acts. These accusations often targeted daycare workers, schoolteachers, and other caretakers, leading to several high-profile trials and widespread hysteria. Although these claims were largely debunked, the moral panic around Satanic rituals and child abuse left a lasting impression on American society. QAnon's narrative of elite child traffickers and Satan-worshipping cabal members revives these fears, adding a layer of horror to the idea of an evil cabal. By connecting political elites with Satanic practices, QAnon taps into the emotional resonance of the Satanic Panic, linking present-day fears of corruption with deeply ingrained anxieties about moral decay and the safety of children.

The Great Awakening also echoes religious themes, particularly within evangelical Christianity, where many followers believe in an "end times" event where good will triumph over evil. In the context of QAnon, the Great Awakening functions as a secular version of an apocalyptic event, a revelation of truth that will set the righteous apart from the corrupt. For many QAnon followers, this narrative mirrors the Christian concept of salvation, where believers are rewarded for their faith and nonbelievers face judgment. Q's messages often use language with religious undertones, framing the movement as a struggle between light and darkness, truth and deception. This religious resonance gives followers a moral foundation for their beliefs and actions, allowing them to see themselves as righteous warriors fighting to save society from destruction.

Another layer of QAnon's Great Awakening is its appeal to a sense of justice and retribution against elites who, followers believe, have gone unpunished for too long. The idea that powerful people operate beyond the law is a common theme in conspiracy theories, but QAnon amplifies this grievance by suggesting that the elites' crimes are not only financial or political but also deeply immoral and inhuman. By painting members of the cabal as child traffickers, abusers, and Satanists, QAnon builds a narrative that goes beyond corruption—it paints elites as monsters, both irredeemable and deserving of the most severe punishments. The Great Awakening promises followers that these elites will finally face justice, offering a powerful catharsis for those who feel disillusioned, powerless, or betrayed by society's leaders.

This apocalyptic vision provides QAnon followers with a simple and emotionally satisfying way to make sense of a complex and often chaotic world. Rather than grappling with the nuances of politics, economics, and social change, followers can attribute societal issues to the existence of a hidden, evil force. The Great Awakening reduces these complexities to a single, digestible narrative: an epic battle between good and evil, with the promise that, in the end, truth will prevail. This framework allows followers to place their faith in the eventual victory of righteousness, making it easier for them to remain committed to the cause even when predictions and timelines fail to materialize. Each setback can be reframed as part of the plan, a necessary deception to protect the mission until the world is ready to wake up.

For QAnon adherents, the Great Awakening is more than just an event to anticipate; it's a mindset, a worldview, and a personal transformation. Followers see themselves as "awake" to the truth, unlike the "sheep" they believe are being deceived by the cabal. This sense of being part of an enlightened minority gives followers a feeling of superiority, fueling a mission to "red-pill" others—convert them to the QAnon worldview. Through this shared journey, the Great Awakening becomes a communal experience, one that unites followers in a sense of purpose, camaraderie, and collective enlightenment. In online communities, followers often talk about the satisfaction of "waking up" friends, family, and strangers, seeing each new believer as evidence that the Great Awakening is unfolding as promised.

In essence, QAnon's Great Awakening is a modern, secular iteration of a classic apocalyptic myth, repackaging ancient fears, moral panics, and messianic hopes for a contemporary audience. It offers a vision of ultimate justice and moral clarity in a world that often feels morally ambiguous and unjust. For followers, this vision gives meaning to the present and hope for the future, providing a sense of agency and purpose in a time of uncertainty. By promising a dramatic reversal where the powerful will be exposed and punished, the Great Awakening gives QAnon followers something to believe in—a narrative that casts them as heroic participants in a cosmic struggle, poised to witness the dawn of a new, righteous era.

4. The Role of Disillusionment in the U.S. Political Climate

The rise of QAnon cannot be separated from the broader disillusionment that had taken root in American society, particularly in the years leading up to 2017. Political polarization, economic anxiety, and a deepening distrust of institutions created an environment in which radical ideas could flourish. QAnon provided a convenient answer to the question haunting many Americans: Why does the world feel broken? Rather than accepting the messy realities of complex societal issues, QAnon offered a clear-cut explanation: a secret cabal was pulling the strings, and the American people were being deliberately misled. This belief resonated with people who felt abandoned, unheard, and betrayed by a system they once trusted.

One of the central forces driving this disillusionment was the increasing polarization of U.S. politics. The 2016 presidential election highlighted and deepened long-standing divisions within American society. Donald Trump's rise to the presidency, largely on a platform that criticized establishment politicians and promised to "drain the swamp," tapped into widespread resentment toward elites, career politicians, and mainstream media. His unorthodox approach and populist rhetoric appealed to those who felt ignored by both major parties. Trump's messaging resonated particularly strongly among his base, who saw his election as a direct challenge to the political status quo. For many QAnon followers, Trump's victory was not just a political shift but a sign of hope—a signal that someone was finally willing to take on the entrenched powers that had kept ordinary Americans marginalized.

QAnon's narrative tapped directly into this political disillusionment by positioning Trump as the central figure in a clandestine battle against the "deep state," a term followers use to describe the shadowy cabal believed to control government and society from behind the scenes. Every challenge Trump faced in office—from media criticism to opposition within Congress—was reinterpreted by QAnon followers as evidence of the deep state's resistance to his reforms. Trump wasn't just facing political opposition; he was, in their eyes, fighting against an embedded network of elites determined to maintain their control. This framing allowed followers to see Trump's presidency not as part of the typical checks and balances of governance, but as an epic struggle between good and evil, with Trump cast as a heroic figure working to liberate America from the grip of corruption.

In addition to political alienation, economic disillusionment also played a major role in QAnon's appeal. Although the U.S. economy had largely recovered from the 2008 financial crisis by 2017, the benefits of this recovery were far from evenly distributed. Wealth inequality in America was at an all-time high, with wages stagnating for many workers even as corporate profits and stock markets soared. This growing economic disparity fostered resentment and a sense of powerlessness among working- and middle-class Americans, many of whom felt they were being left behind while the wealthy grew richer. This frustration with the "system" dovetailed neatly with QAnon's claims that the elites were not only hoarding wealth but actively working to keep the average person down. The theory provided a convenient scapegoat for economic hardship: it wasn't the result of market forces or policy failures but of deliberate manipulation by the cabal.

Adding to this environment of disillusionment was a pervasive distrust of the media. For years, Americans' trust in mainstream media had been steadily declining, with many believing that news outlets served as mouthpieces for political and corporate interests rather than objective sources of information. This skepticism grew stronger as "fake news" became a prominent buzzword during the 2016 election, with accusations of bias and misinformation leveled at both sides of the political spectrum. Trump frequently attacked the media, calling it "the enemy of the people" and accusing outlets of spreading lies to protect elite interests. QAnon adopted this anti-media sentiment, encouraging followers to disregard mainstream news as part of the cabal's disinformation campaign. By rejecting traditional media, followers felt they were stepping outside the mainstream narrative, embracing what they saw as "the truth" uncovered through Q drops and community-driven research.

QAnon's mantra to "do your own research" empowered followers to become their own investigators, reinforcing the idea that the truth was hidden from the public by a complicit media. This DIY approach to information fed into followers' desire to feel in control of their understanding of world events. They no longer had to rely on what they saw as biased reporting; instead, they could piece together Q's clues, discuss findings with like-minded individuals, and reach their own conclusions. The internet provided a near-infinite landscape of resources, much of it unreliable or misleading, but followers saw themselves as uniquely capable of discerning what was real. This process gave them a sense of agency in a world where they often felt powerless, turning them from passive news consumers into active truth-seekers, part of a digital army fighting against the cabal.

QAnon's theories also reflected a broader cultural shift toward skepticism of authority. Many Americans, particularly younger generations, had come to view traditional institutions with suspicion. The financial crisis, government scandals, and widening inequality had eroded faith in established structures. When Q claimed that politicians, business moguls, and even beloved celebrities were in league with the deep state, followers were primed to believe it. This sense of distrust was amplified by social media platforms, which allowed QAnon theories to spread rapidly, creating echo chambers where followers' suspicions were continually reinforced.

In many ways, QAnon filled a void created by disillusionment and alienation, offering its followers a narrative that was both straightforward and emotionally satisfying. It transformed complex social, political, and economic issues into a story of good versus evil, where the cause of all suffering could be attributed to a single, powerful enemy. QAnon gave people an outlet for their frustrations and a sense of belonging to a movement that promised to restore justice and truth. For followers, it wasn't just a theory—it was a cause, a way to reclaim control in a world that felt chaotic and hostile.

Through QAnon, followers found meaning and purpose, a unifying story that explained their struggles and allowed them to see themselves as warriors for a righteous cause. This sense of shared mission made it difficult for many to let go of the theory, even in the face of contradictory evidence. For those disillusioned with the current state of society, QAnon provided a framework through which they could interpret events, a lens that turned their discontent into a call for action. By tapping into America's existing fractures and anxieties, QAnon was able to create a powerful narrative that resonated deeply with those who felt left behind, offering them a sense of empowerment in a world that had otherwise made them feel small and insignificant.

5. The Digital Soldiers: Early Followers and Their Role

From the outset, QAnon was not simply a conspiracy theory to be passively observed—it was a call to action. Q's cryptic posts invited followers to become "digital soldiers," warriors in an information war to expose hidden truths and awaken the masses. This concept transformed the QAnon movement from a fringe theory into an active, engaged community. Early followers, often referred to as "anons," took it upon themselves to analyze, decode, and spread Q's messages, building a culture of collaboration and shared purpose that quickly solidified QAnon's place in the digital landscape. In this way, followers were not just consumers of QAnon content; they were creators and participants, fully immersed in a collective mission they believed was of historical importance.

One of Q's most frequent instructions to followers was to "do your own research." This seemingly simple directive empowered followers to become investigators, piecing together what they saw as clues in Q's posts to uncover the truth. This call to action provided followers with a sense of agency, as they took on the role of independent researchers unearthing hidden information. Online, they delved into every Q drop, meticulously examining each word, phrase, and symbol for possible meanings. This process of "decoding" gave rise to a participatory experience akin to solving a mystery. Followers formed communities on forums like 8chan, Reddit, and later, social media platforms like Twitter, Facebook, and YouTube, where they shared their findings, discussed interpretations, and developed theories together. This group analysis was known as "baking" Q's drops, a process where fragments of information were assembled into a coherent narrative that became the bedrock of QAnon's beliefs.

As digital soldiers, followers felt a profound sense of responsibility and purpose. They saw themselves as the only ones who could see the truth, members of a special group chosen to spread awareness and awaken others. Many adopted the motto "WWG1WGA"—"Where We Go One, We Go All"—a phrase that became synonymous with QAnon and underscored the movement's ethos of loyalty and unity. Through social media, QAnon followers spread the word far and wide, sharing Q drops, crafting memes, creating videos, and adopting hashtags to expand the movement's reach. These efforts turned QAnon into a highly visible digital phenomenon, moving from the anonymity of internet message boards into mainstream platforms where new followers were constantly recruited. The digital soldiers' role wasn't just to believe in QAnon but to actively evangelize it, creating a self-perpetuating cycle that kept the movement alive and growing.

Among these digital soldiers, certain followers emerged as influencers and interpreters, gaining large followings of their own within the QAnon community. These individuals became trusted voices, providing interpretations of Q drops, offering theories, and reinforcing key messages. Many of these influencers capitalized on their popularity by creating YouTube channels, podcasts, and social media accounts dedicated to QAnon, where they translated the often cryptic language of Q's posts for a broader audience. They became, in a sense, lieutenants in QAnon's information war, bridging the gap between Q's obscure messages and the average follower's understanding. For followers, these influencers served as guides, helping them make sense of an increasingly complex and sprawling narrative. Some influencers even went so far as to claim insider knowledge, adding layers of credibility and intrigue to their interpretations.

The movement's sense of purpose only grew as digital soldiers took QAnon's message offline. Followers began attending Trump rallies and political events, often sporting QAnon merchandise or displaying signs with Q-related slogans. The movement's iconography, like the letter "Q" or the WWG1WGA motto, became visible symbols of loyalty to the cause and recognition among followers. Public gatherings became rallying points, reinforcing the idea that QAnon was not only an online phenomenon but a real-world movement. By showing up at political events, followers felt they were sending a message to the world and the cabal—that they were here, aware, and ready to fight. For many, attending these events provided a sense of community and solidarity, further cementing their commitment to QAnon's mission.

The role of QAnon's digital soldiers took on a life of its own, as followers organized and coordinated to spread their message. Social media algorithms, which tend to amplify sensational content, played a significant role in spreading QAnon narratives far beyond their original forums. QAnon's digital soldiers became adept at using these algorithms to their advantage, creating memes and videos designed to go viral, often using hashtags that co-opted mainstream movements, such as #SaveTheChildren, to attract people outside the community. This tactic not only grew the movement but also lent it an air of legitimacy by associating QAnon's goals with genuine causes. The digital soldiers became masters of leveraging the internet's architecture, pushing QAnon's content to new audiences and drawing in followers who might otherwise have never encountered the theory.

For the digital soldiers, QAnon was more than a conspiracy theory; it was a way of life. Their shared mission fostered a strong sense of identity and belonging, a bond strengthened by the perception that they were fighting a righteous battle against a powerful enemy. In their eyes, they were not just internet users but warriors in a digital revolution, united by a purpose greater than themselves. This commitment made it difficult for followers to disengage, as they saw their work not only as uncovering the truth but as safeguarding society from corruption and evil. As they worked together to decode Q's messages and spread the word, digital soldiers felt like part of an epic struggle, a chosen few standing against a global conspiracy.

QAnon's digital soldiers were the engine driving the movement forward, using the internet to transform a series of anonymous posts into a sprawling, real-world movement. By turning followers into participants, Q created a movement that was self-sustaining and constantly expanding. Followers didn't just consume QAnon's ideas; they actively propagated them, creating a feedback loop that amplified the movement's reach and resilience. Through their dedication and digital savvy, QAnon's followers transformed from ordinary citizens into a network of digital activists, convinced they were playing a vital role in a struggle for truth and justice. The identity of the digital soldier became a badge of honor within the movement, binding followers to the cause and to each other, ensuring that QAnon would endure, regardless of whether the prophecies came true.

Chapter 4: Q's Followers and Digital Soldiers

1. The Birth of Digital Soldiers: Motivations and Identity

In the dim, anonymous expanse of the internet, a new kind of army was forming—an army without guns, uniforms, or borders. They called themselves "digital soldiers," and their battleground was the endless web of message boards, social media platforms, and chat rooms. To the uninitiated, they might seem like just another group of conspiracy theorists clinging to strange beliefs. But for these followers, QAnon was more than a theory; it was a mission, a purpose, a reason to fight against forces they believed were destroying society from within. And, as they saw it, they were the last line of defense in a hidden war for humanity's soul.

Followers were drawn to QAnon for different reasons, but most shared a deep sense of disillusionment with the world around them. Many felt betrayed by the institutions they'd once trusted—the government, the media, the education system. The stories of corruption, deceit, and scandal that seemed to cycle endlessly through the news left them jaded and skeptical. Life felt chaotic, and there was a gnawing sense that something, somewhere, had gone terribly wrong.

Then came Q, an anonymous figure dropping clues from behind the scenes, promising answers and a hidden truth.

Q didn't give them the truth outright. Instead, Q offered cryptic clues, scattered like breadcrumbs, and asked them to follow. "Do your own research," Q would say, a call that sparked something within followers. Finally, here was a movement that wasn't just about listening to someone else's version of reality—it was about finding it out for themselves. This was more than consuming information; it was actively participating in a discovery, digging into secrets that others couldn't or wouldn't see. It was empowering.

For those who felt isolated, angry, or alienated, QAnon provided a community that promised to uncover the truth. This was a place where questioning the mainstream wasn't just accepted but celebrated. And followers quickly adopted the identity of "digital soldiers," as if taking an oath to uncover and fight against the hidden evil they believed was poisoning society. The term "Where We Go One, We Go All"—WWG1WGA—became their rallying cry, a phrase that signaled unity and purpose, reminding them that they were not alone in their quest.

The digital soldier identity gave followers a sense of belonging. Here, in this community, they found others who shared their suspicions, their frustrations, their hopes. Their mission wasn't easy; the clues were often cryptic, the information overwhelming, but that only heightened the sense of adventure. They saw themselves as part of a larger, righteous cause, warriors in a shadow war, fighting not with guns but with information. They shared tips on forums, discussed theories, and encouraged each other to keep digging. Every new Q drop felt like a step closer to a hidden truth that only they could uncover.

For the digital soldiers, QAnon was more than an online obsession. It was a purpose, a new lens through which they saw the world and themselves. They weren't just reading about a conspiracy—they were living it, fighting for it. The mission gave meaning to their lives, and as they logged into their forums each day, they knew they weren't just browsing the internet. They were stepping into a battle, united by a promise to expose the lies, no matter how deeply they ran. And to each other, they whispered their creed: "Where We Go One, We Go All."

2. Decoding Q Drops: The Process and Appeal of Gamified Conspiracy

Each new message from Q arrived like a puzzle piece, dropped into the digital world without explanation or context. There were no step-by-step instructions, no clear guide to decipher what Q's cryptic phrases meant. But that was part of the allure. For followers, these "Q drops" were the ultimate scavenger hunt, a series of breadcrumbs leading toward a hidden truth that only the truly dedicated could see. Every post was deliberately vague, sometimes a question—"Who controls the media?"—other times a statement that seemed to border on prophecy: "The storm is upon us. Trust the plan." The meanings were slippery, never obvious, as if waiting for someone to unlock them.

Followers who logged onto their forums felt like they were diving into the unknown, a world of codes, symbols, and secrets waiting to be unraveled. They called the process of analyzing Q drops "baking," as if each clue were an ingredient that needed to be mixed, refined, and cooked until the final product—a revelation—was ready. Together, they worked, sifting through every letter, every punctuation mark, looking for hidden meanings. Some even analyzed timestamps and patterns, convinced that Q's posts contained layers upon layers of hidden significance.

The act of decoding became an almost religious ritual, a ceremony that took hours, even days, to complete. Threads swelled with theories, with followers sharing interpretations, offering insights, and challenging each other. One user might suggest that Q's reference to "the storm" pointed to an impending political upheaval, while another argued it was a signal for something even grander—perhaps the long-awaited arrests of the cabal members they believed controlled the world. Some took to cross-referencing old posts with new ones, spotting what they believed to be coded messages meant only for those paying close attention.

Decoding Q drops gave followers a sense of intellectual superiority. Here, they weren't just reading a theory; they were discovering it, assembling it from fragments of clues in a way that no one else could. They believed they were seeing patterns that ordinary people missed, uncovering the secrets hidden in plain sight. It was a thrilling experience, a rush of empowerment that made them feel like part of an elite team of investigators, pulling back the curtain on a world controlled by shadowy elites. Each solved clue felt like a personal victory, another step closer to exposing the lies they believed society was built on.

But it wasn't just about finding the answer. The process itself was addictive, a kind of gamified reality that rewarded them with bursts of excitement each time they connected the dots. Q drops were like breadcrumbs leading them deeper into the forest, and the journey was just as important as the destination. The community around them fueled the thrill, with users sharing "Eureka!" moments and congratulating each other on making new connections. It was a cooperative game, one that gave them a sense of unity and shared purpose. Together, they felt as if they were unraveling a great mystery, a hidden truth that would one day change the world.

Over time, the act of decoding Q drops became as important as the drops themselves. Followers would eagerly await each new message, logging in at odd hours just to see if Q had posted again. The anticipation, the buildup, and the shared thrill of discovery kept them coming back, fueling a cycle that only grew stronger with each new clue. In the process, they became deeply invested, both in the theories they were building and in the digital community around them. This wasn't just an online pastime; it was a mission, a shared quest where every follower was a vital player, every Q drop a step closer to the truth.

The mysteries woven into each Q drop became the lifeblood of the community, bonding followers through shared effort and belief. Decoding wasn't easy—often, it was a frustrating, labyrinthine process. But each solved riddle, each hint that seemed to reveal something more, reinforced their sense of purpose. For the digital soldiers, it wasn't enough to believe in Q's message; they had to live it, to decode it, to prove that they, too, were worthy of knowing the hidden truths. And as they pieced together Q's riddles, they felt a collective thrill, a spark of insight that only they, the awakened few, could understand.

3. Spreading the Message: Social Media and the Echo Chamber

Once they'd decoded the latest Q drop and debated its meaning on forums, the digital soldiers took to the wider web to spread what they believed was the truth. Social media became their battlefield, a place where each tweet, post, and hashtag was a weapon wielded in the war against the "cabal" they believed controlled the world. Platforms like Twitter, Facebook, and YouTube offered them a megaphone, amplifying their voices and pushing their message far beyond the insular boards of 4chan and 8chan. With each post, they reached new eyes, planting seeds of curiosity and doubt in people who might never have come across QAnon otherwise.

Hashtags became essential tools. "#WWG1WGA" and "#TrustThePlan" were rallying cries that united followers and drew in newcomers. But it was "#SaveTheChildren" that gained the most traction, co-opting a genuine humanitarian cause and cloaking the movement in a mantle of righteous concern. By associating their beliefs with the fight against child trafficking—a universally condemned crime—they blurred the lines between legitimate activism and conspiracy theory. Posts bearing the hashtag flooded social media, with users sharing emotionally charged images and warnings about elite child-trafficking rings. For many followers, every share, like, and retweet was a step toward waking up the public. They believed they were rescuing innocents, exposing darkness, and making a real difference in the world.

Social media's algorithms only amplified the movement's reach. Designed to promote content that sparked engagement, these algorithms favored the sensational, the shocking, and the extreme—exactly the kind of material QAnon thrived on. Posts that played on people's fears, particularly when related to child safety, quickly went viral, crossing the threshold from fringe communities into the feeds of ordinary people. Followers would share videos, conspiracy theories, and memes that packaged complex ideas into digestible—and shareable—snippets. The digital soldiers saw themselves as missionaries, spreading "truth" to an unsuspecting world, and each viral post felt like a small victory, another blow struck against the cabal.

The more followers engaged on social media, the more they found themselves surrounded by like-minded believers, forming an echo chamber that reinforced their beliefs. Each day, their feeds filled with posts from other QAnon followers, reaffirming the movement's core ideas and adding new theories to the ever-growing web of Q's cryptic messages. The posts of dissenters or fact-checkers were quickly dismissed as "fake news" or cabal propaganda, further insulating followers from outside perspectives. Over time, this environment made it easy to believe that the movement was larger than it was. For them, it seemed like everyone was finally waking up, the evidence all around them in the comments, retweets, and shares from people who were just as convinced.

Within this digital echo chamber, conspiracy theories that would have been easily dismissed in the real world gained legitimacy. As followers shared and re-shared each other's content, fringe ideas became mainstream within the community. The lack of outside perspectives created a feedback loop, where followers fed off one another's energy and escalated one another's beliefs. What might have started as a casual interest quickly deepened into a conviction, as the constant exposure to QAnon content made even the most outlandish ideas seem possible. In these online spaces, doubts faded, replaced by a collective certainty that they alone saw the truth.

Their collective reach didn't go unnoticed. As the movement grew, mainstream media outlets began reporting on QAnon, drawing attention to the conspiracy theories spreading through social media. For the digital soldiers, this was proof that they were being heard and that their work was making an impact. But they interpreted the media's critical coverage as evidence that the cabal was worried, that the powers-that-be were trying to suppress the truth. Each article dismissing QAnon only fueled their sense of mission, deepening their distrust in the press and strengthening their resolve to spread the message.

Through social media, the digital soldiers found not only a platform but a mission field, a place where they could take their beliefs from the depths of obscure message boards to the public sphere. Every post, every share, every hashtag was a small rebellion, an act of defiance against what they saw as a corrupt and controlling system. In their minds, they weren't just followers of a conspiracy theory; they were warriors of truth, connecting with strangers, spreading what they believed was the reality hidden beneath the surface. Each day, they logged in, scrolled, and shared, bound together in their mission and ready to take on the digital world.

4. Influencers and Interpreters: The Rise of Key Voices

As QAnon gained momentum, certain figures emerged from the crowd, individuals who became voices of authority within the movement. These influencers were skilled at interpreting Q's cryptic drops, transforming vague clues into powerful, persuasive narratives. On YouTube channels, podcasts, and social media accounts, they would break down the latest Q drops, offering followers theories, explanations, and encouragement to keep faith in "the plan." In a movement built on ambiguity, these interpreters became trusted guides, providing clarity and direction in the labyrinthine world of QAnon.

For followers, these influencers held a unique status, revered as voices who seemed to "get it"—people who could decipher Q's messages with remarkable insight. Some of these figures were ordinary people with newfound online fame, while others had backgrounds in media or politics that lent an air of credibility. They took on the role of teachers, breaking down Q's messages line by line, connecting dots, and drawing inferences that followers could rally behind. To the digital soldiers, these influencers were almost prophetic figures, able to see the big picture in ways others could not. Their interpretations became gospel within the community, guiding how followers understood Q's messages and shaping the movement's overall direction.

A handful of influencers rose to particular prominence, amassing large followings and becoming celebrities in their own right within the QAnon ecosystem. With their loyal audiences, these influencers were able to monetize their roles, asking for donations, selling merchandise, or creating subscriber-only content. Some even organized live streams, where thousands of followers would tune in, hanging on their every word, eager to know what the latest Q drop might mean. The more enigmatic Q's posts, the more followers relied on these influencers to decode them, and the larger their followings grew. With that influence came power, and with power, a responsibility to maintain the narrative and keep followers invested.

These influencers carefully curated their public personas, often adopting the language of patriotism and faith. They spoke about a divine mission, a righteous struggle against evil, and the need to "stay strong" in the face of mounting criticism. Many leaned heavily into religious language, framing the movement as a battle between good and evil, with themselves as faithful guides on the path to truth. This framing resonated deeply with followers, many of whom already viewed the world in moral and spiritual terms. The influencers' words provided reassurance, an anchor in the storm, and for many, a feeling of certainty in an uncertain world.

But their influence extended beyond merely interpreting Q's messages. Over time, these figures began shaping the movement, introducing their own theories and embellishments to the core ideas of QAnon. Some speculated on timelines, hinting at dates when "the storm" might come and justice would finally be served. Others connected the dots between Q's drops and current events, convincing followers that every major headline was part of Q's grand plan. As these influencers' interpretations filtered through the movement, they took on a life of their own, adding layers to QAnon's mythology and sometimes even overshadowing Q's original messages. For followers, the influencers' words carried as much weight as Q's posts, and in some cases, even more.

The sense of authority these influencers held within QAnon was profound. Followers trusted them not only to interpret Q drops but to guide them on a personal level, answering their questions, addressing their doubts, and keeping them engaged with the movement. In private Facebook groups, on Twitter, and through direct messages, they would reassure anxious followers, telling them to "trust the plan" and keep the faith. This personal connection deepened followers' loyalty, making it harder for them to question the movement or walk away. For many, these influencers were not just interpreters but mentors, people they felt connected to on a deeply personal level.

In time, the influencers became indispensable to the QAnon ecosystem, voices of authority that followers looked to for guidance, reassurance, and meaning. They shaped the movement's narrative, turning Q's cryptic messages into a coherent story that could be understood and followed. For the digital soldiers, these influencers were the torchbearers, illuminating the path forward, giving them direction, and ensuring they would remain loyal to the cause. Through their words, they transformed QAnon from a series of disjointed clues into a story of purpose and promise, a story that made sense of a chaotic world and assured followers they were on the right side of history.

5. Real-World Impact: From Digital Activism to Public Demonstrations

For the digital soldiers, spreading QAnon's message online was only the beginning. As their ranks grew, so did their sense of mission, and the movement that started in the depths of internet message boards began spilling over into the real world. Followers showed up at Trump rallies, political events, and public gatherings, proudly displaying QAnon symbols, slogans, and homemade signs. The letter "Q" adorned T-shirts, hats, and banners, and chants of "Where We Go One, We Go All" rang out in unison, each follower feeling part of something greater than themselves. They were no longer just a virtual community—they were a visible force, bringing Q's message out of cyberspace and into the streets.

At these events, QAnon followers felt a renewed sense of solidarity and strength. Surrounded by others who shared their beliefs, they didn't feel like a fringe group but like a movement poised to reveal the hidden truths they believed everyone needed to hear. People gathered in small clusters, sharing theories, handing out flyers, and exchanging tips on how to "wake up" more people. For many, it was the first time they'd connected face-to-face with others who truly understood them, who shared their conviction that they were part of a historic struggle. Together, they felt validated, as if they were on the front lines of a battle for the country's soul, a struggle between good and evil.

At Trump rallies, QAnon symbols and slogans blended seamlessly with the red, white, and blue of MAGA hats and American flags. Q followers saw these rallies as a unique opportunity to connect with like-minded people, to recruit new believers, and to show their support for the president they believed was leading the fight against the cabal. They held up signs that read, "Q Sent Me" and "Trust the Plan," displaying their loyalty proudly. Often, they would nod or exchange knowing glances when they spotted someone else wearing the "Q," a silent affirmation that they were part of something extraordinary. For followers, these events were more than political gatherings—they were moments of revelation, proof that they were not alone in their beliefs.

But as the movement's presence grew, so did its impact, and QAnon followers began to take more direct actions. Convinced that they were fighting to save children from an elite trafficking ring, some followers took it upon themselves to act, tracking down supposed "cabal" members, posting their personal information online, or showing up at businesses they believed were part of the conspiracy. Real-world harassment became an unfortunate consequence of QAnon's spread, with some followers harassing public figures, activists, and even private citizens they believed were linked to the cabal. In the minds of the digital soldiers, they were defending the innocent, taking a stand against a corrupt system that had gone unchecked for too long.

Over time, the QAnon movement began organizing its own rallies, attracting followers from around the country who felt compelled to take their message beyond the screen. These gatherings served as recruitment drives, public demonstrations, and community-building events all rolled into one. People of all ages and backgrounds, drawn together by their shared mission, carried signs declaring "Save the Children" or "The Great Awakening is Here." Speakers took to makeshift stages to share their stories of "waking up" to the truth, urging others to spread the message to friends and family. The passion was palpable—these were people who believed, beyond a shadow of a doubt, that they were fighting for humanity's future.

As QAnon became more visible, its presence and messaging became harder for the mainstream to ignore. News reports and social media discussions began to highlight the movement's real-world actions, drawing attention to the conspiracy theory that had once lived in the shadows. Some QAnon followers saw this coverage as confirmation of their cause, interpreting any negative attention as evidence of the cabal's fear. To them, every article condemning the movement, every social media crackdown, was proof that they were getting closer to the truth. The more they were criticized, the more convinced they became that they were on the right path.

In the eyes of QAnon's digital soldiers, these rallies and public actions were the beginning of the Great Awakening they'd been waiting for, the first rumblings of a shift that would soon expose the cabal and redeem society. They saw themselves as prophets and warriors, ready to lead the world into a new era of truth. The line between the online world and the real world had blurred, and the QAnon movement was no longer just a digital phenomenon. It was alive, tangible, with followers who believed that their actions were bringing the day of reckoning ever closer.

For the digital soldiers, the mission was no longer confined to keyboards and screens. They had stepped out into the world, faces uncovered, symbols displayed, marching for a cause that had given them purpose. In their hearts, they believed that their efforts would one day be vindicated, that history would remember them as the ones who dared to fight back. And so, with flags waving and signs held high, they marched forward, determined to bring about the change they believed was inevitable, one step closer to the world they envisioned, where the truth would finally be known.

Chapter 5: The Appeal of QAnon

1. **The Allure of Secret Knowledge: Being "In the Know"**
QAnon's promise of hidden, exclusive knowledge is one of its most powerful draws. For followers, Q's cryptic messages aren't just conspiracy theories—they are keys to unlocking a hidden reality. Each Q drop is presented as a piece of insider information, written in a code that only the truly "awake" can decipher. To followers, these messages are more than words on a screen; they are revelations, hints leading them down a rabbit hole to the truth that others are too blind, or too controlled, to see. QAnon offers them a sense of enlightenment that allows them to feel special, set apart from the masses still "asleep" to the world's true workings.

The appeal of secret knowledge taps into a deep psychological desire: the need to understand the unknown, to uncover secrets that seem just out of reach. QAnon followers are promised access to information that goes far beyond what the media, government, or even their own communities provide. They believe they are being let in on the world's biggest secrets—the real reasons behind political events, societal unrest, and even natural disasters. For them, the power players of the world are manipulating society from behind closed doors, and only those who follow Q have the ability to see through the illusion.

Q's messages are crafted to reinforce this sense of enlightenment. The cryptic language—"Trust the plan," "The storm is upon us," "Where We Go One, We Go All"—is filled with double meanings and references that make followers feel as though they're reading between the lines, glimpsing truths that the rest of society is too naive or brainwashed to perceive. By interpreting these messages, followers feel like they're peeling back layers of deception, piecing together a grand conspiracy one cryptic phrase at a time. This process transforms each Q drop into a puzzle, and with each solved riddle, followers feel they're proving their own intelligence, intuition, and insight.

The allure of hidden knowledge has historically been at the core of many conspiracy theories, and QAnon is no different. Throughout history, secret societies, hidden agendas, and shadow governments have captivated those who feel that the official version of events doesn't add up. The promise of "seeing beyond the veil" is a powerful one, giving followers a sense of superiority, as if they alone possess the true version of reality. To them, understanding Q's messages sets them apart from the "sheep"—the unawakened masses who blindly follow mainstream narratives without question.

For QAnon followers, the pursuit of secret knowledge is not just an intellectual exercise; it becomes a core part of their identity. By aligning themselves with Q, they join an exclusive community of "truth seekers" who feel as though they are saving humanity from ignorance. Every new piece of information, every decoded Q drop, reinforces this sense of enlightenment. It creates a bond between followers, a shared understanding that they are in possession of a hidden truth, a truth that has the power to change the world if only enough people could wake up and see it. In their minds, they're not just bystanders; they are guardians of a secret that has the potential to expose the powerful and reshape society.

This allure of secret knowledge is a potent psychological force, pulling followers deeper into the movement. It fosters a sense of superiority, certainty, and self-worth, fueling their dedication to the cause. And as they share their insights and connect with others, they feel a growing confidence in their understanding of the world—a feeling of being "in the know" that becomes difficult to let go, regardless of evidence or reality. For QAnon's digital soldiers, the pursuit of hidden truths is more than a pastime; it's a mission, a revelation, a path that gives them clarity, purpose, and belonging in a world they see as veiled in darkness.

2. Sense of Purpose: A Mission Against Evil

For QAnon followers, this isn't just a conspiracy theory—it's a crusade. The movement doesn't merely offer followers explanations for the world's problems; it gives them a clear enemy and a role in an epic struggle. They aren't just consuming Q's messages passively; they are "digital soldiers" on a mission to expose and defeat what they believe is a cabal of corrupt elites committing heinous crimes. The idea of being part of this righteous battle against evil gives followers a profound sense of purpose, transforming them from ordinary people into warriors of truth.

QAnon's messaging emphasizes the stakes in stark terms: society is under threat, and only the faithful, the truly "awake," can help save it. This mission is presented as nothing less than the defense of humanity itself, with followers called to fight for the innocent, particularly children, who they believe are being harmed by powerful figures. In this narrative, followers are not only protectors but avengers, bringing justice to those who have been victimized. This sense of duty and righteousness provides an emotional anchor, an intense feeling of moral clarity that makes the movement deeply compelling.

The concept of the Great Awakening, a promised event in which the truth will be revealed and justice will be served, adds another layer to this sense of purpose. Followers believe that one day, the world will "wake up" and see the truths they have been fighting to expose. They imagine a reckoning—a moment when all the evildoers will be brought to justice, and society will be restored to a state of moral clarity. For them, this isn't just a vague hope; it's an inevitability, something they are working to bring about through their efforts. Every post, every meme, every decoded message is a step closer to this prophesied moment, reinforcing their commitment to the cause.

In this war between good and evil, followers see themselves as the heroes, with Q as their guiding light. The narrative of QAnon elevates their actions beyond personal interest, framing each post, each shared video, as a blow against the forces of darkness. This transformation of everyday people into "soldiers" and "guardians" is empowering. Many followers have ordinary, often unremarkable lives, filled with the frustrations and uncertainties that most people experience. QAnon offers them a chance to transcend the ordinary, to take on a role that feels vital and grand. In fighting for Q's mission, they gain not just a purpose but a sense of heroism—a feeling that they are on the right side of history, working to expose hidden corruption and bring about a better world.

This sense of purpose also provides followers with a way to channel their anger, frustration, and fears into something they view as constructive. For those who feel marginalized or alienated, QAnon is more than an ideology; it's an outlet, a way to act on their dissatisfaction with society. Instead of feeling powerless in the face of world events, they now feel as though they're taking part in shaping history, defending innocence, and exposing lies. Their belief in a noble cause gives them strength, allowing them to see their sacrifices—whether they're personal relationships, reputation, or time—as necessary contributions to the greater good.

In the end, QAnon's promise of purpose is one of its strongest appeals. The movement gives followers something to believe in, a reason to wake up each morning, and a community of like-minded people who share in that purpose. For many, it fills a void, a need to feel part of something larger than themselves. In the fight against a cabal they believe controls the world, QAnon followers have found a purpose that feels uniquely theirs, a sense of mission that transforms their ordinary lives into a story of heroism, sacrifice, and ultimate redemption.

3. "Doing Your Own Research": Empowerment and Self-Discovery

One of QAnon's most powerful hooks is its call for followers to "do your own research." This mantra, repeated across Q's messages, offers followers an invitation to take control of their understanding of the world. Unlike traditional media sources, which present information to be accepted at face value, QAnon encourages followers to look beyond the mainstream, to dig deeper, to uncover "truths" that only they have the initiative to find. For many, this is exhilarating; it turns them from passive recipients of information into active investigators. This self-guided research becomes a badge of honor, a sign that they are intellectually independent, part of an elite group brave enough to seek knowledge for themselves.

Followers approach this research with the zeal of detectives on a grand case, combing through articles, analyzing news events, and cross-referencing Q's cryptic "drops" with current headlines. Each Q drop becomes a piece of evidence in a sprawling, intricate puzzle, and followers relish the challenge of piecing it together. They scour obscure websites, forums, and videos, constructing elaborate timelines, connecting dots, and building what they believe is a comprehensive understanding of world events. This process of decoding isn't just mentally engaging—it's profoundly empowering. With each connection made, followers feel they are gaining insight, elevating themselves above the "asleep" masses who unquestioningly accept mainstream narratives.

The act of research within QAnon isn't just about learning; it's about constructing a personalized reality. Followers are given the freedom to interpret Q's messages in ways that feel significant to them, blending current events, personal beliefs, and fragments of information into a coherent worldview. This process becomes highly rewarding, a self-fulfilling loop where every "discovery" reinforces their belief in QAnon's core tenets. Rather than dissuading them, contradictions or gaps in logic often lead to deeper levels of analysis, as followers reinterpret Q's cryptic clues in ways that suit their own narratives. For many, this feeling of intellectual freedom is addictive; the more they decode, the more they feel they're uncovering a truth the world refuses to see.

Beyond the intellectual satisfaction, doing one's own research also brings a sense of control in a world that feels chaotic and unpredictable. As global crises, political turmoil, and economic challenges mount, QAnon followers find solace in feeling that they have a unique handle on reality. They believe they understand the hidden forces driving world events, allowing them to make sense of an otherwise bewildering world. In this way, QAnon offers more than information—it provides a framework that followers can rely on, a way to process events that otherwise might seem random or overwhelming. This perceived control brings comfort, making followers feel more secure and prepared in a world that often feels out of their grasp.

This emphasis on self-research also sets QAnon apart from traditional institutions, reinforcing followers' belief that they have liberated themselves from mainstream propaganda. QAnon followers view themselves as truth-seekers, unshackled by what they see as the limitations and biases of conventional media. In their eyes, they are not just uncovering hidden information but reclaiming their intellectual freedom from the influences of a "corrupt" media landscape. This self-directed research fosters an air of independence and authenticity within the movement, creating a shared culture of skepticism toward authority that binds followers together.

For QAnon adherents, "doing your own research" is both a rallying cry and a ritual, one that solidifies their loyalty and draws them deeper into the movement. Each hour spent combing through obscure sources, every theory formed from fragmented information, reinforces their commitment to the cause. In time, the act of research becomes almost sacred—a way to prove their devotion, to show that they, too, are fighting to uncover the truth. In their minds, they are not conspiracy theorists; they are researchers, pioneers of truth blazing a trail through the fog of deception. This journey of self-guided discovery becomes a core part of their identity, turning followers into active participants in QAnon's narrative and giving them a sense of purpose, power, and agency that is difficult to abandon.

4. Community and Belonging: The Power of "We"

One of the most compelling aspects of QAnon is the powerful sense of community it offers. For many followers, joining the movement means becoming part of a larger family, a group that shares their beliefs, frustrations, and hopes for the future. In QAnon, they find acceptance, camaraderie, and a space where they feel they belong. It's a community where no one dismisses their ideas, no matter how unusual or unconventional they may seem to outsiders. Instead, followers feel celebrated for their willingness to "think for themselves," forming bonds that transcend geography, age, and background. In a society that often feels fragmented and isolating, QAnon offers a strong and inclusive identity, a sense of "we" that brings followers together.

Online forums, social media groups, and message boards become virtual meeting places where followers can discuss the latest Q drops, share theories, and provide support for one another. These spaces function as echo chambers, where ideas are amplified, reinforced, and celebrated. As followers share stories, decode clues, and connect dots, they create a shared reality that feels as tangible as the physical world around them. The language, symbols, and references unique to QAnon—like "WWG1WGA" or the letter "Q" itself—become markers of inclusion, a shorthand that instantly signals who is part of the "in-group." Followers greet each other as brothers and sisters in arms, united in a common mission and bound by the knowledge they believe only they possess.

This sense of belonging goes beyond intellectual connection; it's deeply emotional. In QAnon communities, followers find people who not only share their beliefs but also validate their fears, frustrations, and doubts. Many have experienced estrangement from friends and family who don't understand or accept their views, and QAnon provides a support system for those who feel misunderstood or rejected by society. Here, they are free to voice concerns that might be dismissed elsewhere, confident that others share the same outlook and are willing to listen. Followers form real friendships within these communities, exchanging messages of encouragement, praying together, and even meeting up at rallies or gatherings to celebrate their shared cause.

This community extends offline, as well. QAnon supporters began organizing rallies, displaying Q symbols at public events, and attending Trump rallies in groups, visibly demonstrating their allegiance to the movement. These real-world gatherings give followers the opportunity to connect face-to-face, to shake hands and exchange stories with people they've only known through screens. For many, attending these events is a moment of profound solidarity. They see themselves as part of a larger army, a visible manifestation of the movement's strength and unity. Every "Q" hat, every T-shirt, every homemade sign becomes a badge of belonging, signaling to the world—and to each other—that they are not alone in their beliefs.

The shared rituals of QAnon, from chanting "Where We Go One, We Go All" to creating and sharing Q-themed content, further deepen followers' bonds. These rituals foster a sense of identity and collective purpose, giving followers the feeling that they are part of something monumental. By participating in these rituals, whether online or offline, followers strengthen their sense of belonging and loyalty to the group. They feel united by a common mission, bonded by a mutual understanding, and empowered by the knowledge that they are part of a movement that, in their eyes, transcends individual lives and impacts the course of history.

For many, the sense of community within QAnon fills a void, offering friendship, acceptance, and a shared mission. Followers who might have once felt isolated now find themselves part of a family, a place where they are valued, supported, and understood. This feeling of unity and belonging is a powerful force, one that keeps followers engaged and loyal to the movement. It's no longer just about the conspiracy theories or the cryptic messages; it's about the people beside them, the bonds formed, the friendships forged, and the belief that they are part of a family fighting for truth. In a world that often feels disconnected and fragmented, QAnon provides a space where followers feel whole, part of a community that they will defend, nurture, and belong to—no matter what.

5. Resilience Against Criticism: "Trust the Plan" and Defending the Belief System

One of QAnon's most fascinating aspects is the remarkable resilience of its followers against criticism and evidence that challenges their beliefs. QAnon isn't just an ideology—it's a worldview, fortified by a set of phrases and frameworks that create a protective shell around the movement. "Trust the plan" is one of Q's most powerful instructions, a simple but profound mantra that urges followers to remain steadfast, no matter what happens. For those who believe, this phrase isn't just advice; it's a commandment. Trusting the plan means believing that everything, even setbacks or contradictions, is part of a grand design that only Q and the digital soldiers understand. It offers comfort, a sense of stability, and a reminder that they are part of something bigger than themselves.

When predictions don't come to pass—such as promised mass arrests or political upheavals—followers don't abandon the movement. Instead, they adapt, reframing missed predictions as "misdirection" or as part of Q's necessary strategy to confuse the enemy. They interpret each delay as a test of their loyalty, a temporary setback that Q has anticipated all along. In this way, cognitive dissonance—the psychological discomfort that arises from holding two conflicting beliefs—becomes manageable. Followers develop explanations that reinforce their faith rather than challenge it. To them, every broken promise is simply a twist in the plot, another way to keep their enemies guessing.

The internal language and ideology of QAnon offer followers a self-reinforcing system that shields them from doubt. Critics and fact-checkers are dismissed as part of the "cabal" or the "deep state," labels that neatly categorize outsiders as either ignorant or corrupt. This "us versus them" mentality further strengthens the group, creating an unbreakable barrier between followers and the rest of the world. When friends or family express concerns, followers see it not as a reason to question QAnon but as proof that the cabal's influence runs deep, that even loved ones are unwittingly brainwashed by mainstream media. For followers, rejecting criticism becomes a reaffirmation of their identity, a sign that they are, indeed, "awake" while others are "asleep."

QAnon's structure also provides followers with a framework to rationalize every contradiction. When presented with contradictory evidence, followers often respond with phrases like "disinformation is necessary," a way to explain away inconsistencies. Q himself suggested that not everything he posts should be taken at face value, implying that some clues are meant to throw off enemies or disguise true intentions. This ambiguity serves a dual purpose: it allows Q to be right, no matter what, and it frees followers to interpret events in a way that aligns with their existing beliefs. This structure ensures that QAnon is a flexible belief system, one that can bend around challenges and retain its followers' loyalty.

The concept of "fake news" plays a crucial role in shielding QAnon from outside scrutiny. Followers are taught to distrust mainstream media, seeing it as a tool of the cabal designed to manipulate the public. This deep-seated skepticism of traditional news sources makes it easy for QAnon to dismiss any information that contradicts their worldview. Even well-researched articles, government reports, and expert analyses are waved away as propaganda. Instead, QAnon offers its followers a parallel media landscape, where "truth" is disseminated by influencers within the movement. Followers trust each other, relying on their community for "the real story," which isolates them further from outside perspectives. Every report critical of QAnon, rather than shaking their beliefs, is seen as validation—a sign that they're rattling the establishment and that the truth is being suppressed.

This protective framework creates a sense of certainty and security, allowing followers to navigate an uncertain world with clarity. It's comforting to have a belief system that explains everything, that leaves no room for ambiguity, and that makes sense of even the most confusing events. QAnon's resilience isn't just about rejecting criticism; it's about finding meaning and stability in a complex, often chaotic world. For followers, trusting the plan, dismissing critics, and insulating themselves from outside information becomes a way to hold on to a reality that feels purposeful and structured.

In the end, QAnon's ability to shield itself from criticism is one of its greatest strengths. This resilience binds followers together, reinforcing their sense of loyalty and devotion to the cause. It ensures that, no matter what happens, the movement will endure, adapting around every obstacle and evolving to fit any situation. For those within QAnon, the belief system becomes more than a collection of ideas; it becomes a fortress, a sanctuary of truth, a community united not just by faith but by the resolve to see it through to the end. In their eyes, they are part of a movement that cannot be shaken, that will one day prove itself to the world, and they hold tight to that vision, defending it against all who would try to tear it down.

Chapter 6: The Impact on U.S. Politics

1. **Shaping Voter Beliefs and Attitudes**

QAnon's influence on American voters goes beyond typical political affiliations or loyalties. By weaving a narrative that pits "good" against "evil," QAnon has reshaped how many of its followers view the government, the media, and traditional authority figures. For followers, this isn't just about supporting one candidate over another; it's about rooting out corruption and saving the nation from a hidden cabal they believe is controlling society. This powerful story has eroded trust in the institutions that have traditionally underpinned American democracy, creating a divide between QAnon believers and those who don't share their worldview.

For many QAnon followers, trust in government has evaporated. The movement's core message—that a secret group of elites controls the world—casts every government action, law, or policy as suspect. Even basic democratic processes, like voting and judicial rulings, are viewed with skepticism. Followers often believe that elections are rigged, court decisions are influenced, and even day-to-day governance is manipulated by unseen powers. As a result, they approach political news not with a question of policy or preference but with a question of truth, wondering not what is best for the country, but who might be hiding the truth from them. In a movement grounded in distrust, traditional governance becomes a battleground for unveiling the "truth."

QAnon's narrative has fueled widespread skepticism, especially around the role of the media. Followers are constantly told by Q and QAnon influencers that mainstream media is complicit in hiding the truth, dismissing any reports that challenge their beliefs as "fake news." This has led to a kind of echo chamber where followers rely solely on alternative news sources or interpretations by trusted influencers within the movement. For them, watching the news or reading a newspaper feels like receiving propaganda from the enemy. This skepticism can seep into nearly every aspect of civic life, making QAnon followers suspicious of anyone who doesn't reinforce their beliefs. The result is a fractured perspective on what constitutes factual information, with many followers dismissing established media as corrupt or biased.

The effects of QAnon's belief system on voter perception extend into how followers view political parties and candidates. For QAnon believers, one side of the political spectrum is not just wrong but morally corrupt, with the movement framing certain politicians as outright villains who must be defeated. Conversely, they see those who align with their beliefs, especially those who support or acknowledge QAnon, as saviors in the battle for America's future. This creates a binary perspective in which political issues are no longer matters of policy debate but are instead seen as good versus evil. This black-and-white worldview has intensified partisan divides, with QAnon followers placing unwavering loyalty behind candidates and public figures they believe are fighting the cabal.

In this climate, political discourse becomes highly polarized. QAnon followers often see themselves as guardians of the truth, charged with exposing lies and awakening the "sleeping" public. Engaging with people who don't share their views can lead to frustration, as they interpret disagreement not as a difference of opinion but as evidence that the other person is part of the problem. This perspective makes compromise difficult, further solidifying ideological divides in communities, families, and workplaces. For many QAnon followers, the stakes are so high that they're unwilling to entertain alternative perspectives or consider evidence that doesn't align with their beliefs. To them, their mission is clear: they are on the side of truth, while anyone who challenges that truth is either misled or morally complicit.

In reshaping how followers perceive government, media, and political affiliation, QAnon has created a powerful new lens through which many Americans view the political landscape. Rather than seeing these institutions as flawed but reformable, QAnon followers are conditioned to view them as corrupt to the core. This mindset has deepened distrust and polarization within the electorate, creating a segment of voters who are difficult to reach through traditional political means. For these followers, voting and political participation are no longer just civic duties; they are acts of resistance against a system they believe is fundamentally broken. And in that resistance, QAnon's hold over their beliefs and attitudes remains strong, influencing not only how they vote but how they view their role in the democratic process.

2. QAnon's Role in Political Polarization

QAnon's influence has profoundly deepened political polarization in the United States, creating stark divisions not only between parties but also within them. The movement's ideology frames every issue, event, and political figure through a lens of absolute good versus absolute evil, leaving little room for compromise or middle ground. For QAnon followers, politics is not about policy differences or debates on governance—it's a battle for the soul of the nation. This perspective has led to an "us versus them" mentality that fuels mistrust, antagonism, and, in some cases, outright hostility toward those with differing viewpoints.

The "us versus them" framework inherent in QAnon's messaging transforms politics from a dialogue into a crusade. Followers view themselves as part of a righteous group who have awakened to the truth, while everyone else is either "asleep" or actively complicit in the alleged corruption of society. This mentality places QAnon followers in opposition not only to traditional opponents but also to those who simply don't buy into the movement's worldview. As a result, conversations around policy or political philosophy quickly become combative, with followers seeing any disagreement as a moral failing or a sign of ignorance. This combative stance doesn't just polarize people along partisan lines—it creates a complete chasm, where engaging with opposing viewpoints is seen as unnecessary or even dangerous.

QAnon's "in-group" mentality has led to the creation of isolated echo chambers, both online and offline, where followers surround themselves exclusively with like-minded individuals. Online forums, social media groups, and alternative news sources reinforce QAnon's narratives and create spaces where differing opinions are dismissed or mocked. In these echo chambers, misinformation can thrive unchecked, and fringe ideas gain legitimacy simply because they're repeated and validated by other followers. This self-reinforcing environment heightens followers' loyalty to the movement, as it provides constant validation and further separates them from the perspectives of mainstream society. It solidifies their belief that they, and they alone, see the truth, creating a bond that both isolates and empowers them.

This polarization extends beyond the followers themselves, influencing the broader political discourse. As QAnon followers adopt extreme positions on issues like child trafficking, government surveillance, and the integrity of elections, these ideas seep into mainstream discussions, either through social media amplification or the actions of QAnon-aligned public figures. For example, QAnon's fixation on supposed elite involvement in child trafficking has led to a surge of public discussions on the topic, but often in ways that distort reality and spread misinformation. These narratives make it difficult to have nuanced conversations, as any attempt to fact-check or challenge QAnon's claims is quickly labeled as part of a cover-up, further dividing people and intensifying the movement's distrust of outside voices.

QAnon's impact on political polarization is also evident in how followers respond to mainstream political leaders and public figures who denounce the movement. QAnon's followers frequently dismiss criticism as further proof that their beliefs are correct, believing that anyone who doesn't support the movement's aims is either "part of the cabal" or unwittingly brainwashed. This dismissal creates a wall between QAnon followers and the rest of society, leaving little room for dialogue. It doesn't matter if critics are family members, friends, or lifelong political allies—if they're not fully supportive of QAnon's mission, they're viewed with suspicion and hostility. This rejection of dissenting voices hardens political and personal divides, fragmenting communities and straining personal relationships.

As QAnon followers continue to insulate themselves from opposing viewpoints and interact primarily within the movement, they drift further from conventional political discourse. In the minds of QAnon adherents, they are not merely citizens engaging in democratic debate; they are soldiers in an information war, fighting against a corrupt establishment that they believe is embedded in every part of society. This mindset not only intensifies partisan divides but also creates entirely separate realities, where followers' beliefs become impermeable to fact-checking or dialogue. For the wider political landscape, this polarization is a formidable challenge, as QAnon's presence complicates efforts to find common ground, address public concerns, and maintain a sense of shared truth.

In the end, QAnon's influence on political polarization isn't just about dividing people into different camps; it's about redefining the nature of political identity itself. For followers, QAnon isn't a political stance or even a worldview—it's a totalizing identity, one that shapes how they interact with everyone around them. This identity makes compromise difficult, dialogue strained, and reconciliation nearly impossible. The movement's insistence on a binary, morally charged view of politics has made QAnon a powerful force in deepening divides, reshaping how people engage with politics, and fragmenting the political landscape into isolated factions, each increasingly skeptical of the other.

3. Influence on Elections and Campaign Strategies

QAnon's influence on American elections has extended far beyond online communities, shaping campaign strategies, candidate platforms, and voter mobilization in unprecedented ways. While QAnon initially grew in the shadows of internet message boards, its reach has since expanded, finding supporters within the political mainstream. Candidates have increasingly used—or in some cases, subtly referenced—QAnon rhetoric, realizing that openly aligning with the movement can secure a loyal, highly engaged voting bloc. This has had a ripple effect, influencing not only local and state races but also national campaigns and changing the landscape of American electoral politics.

In recent election cycles, several candidates have leaned into QAnon's language, symbols, and themes to appeal to a base that feels alienated by traditional politics. This strategy often involves adopting QAnon's rhetoric about "fighting the deep state" or "draining the swamp," code phrases that resonate deeply with QAnon followers. Even candidates who don't explicitly endorse QAnon often hint at alignment by invoking themes that overlap with the movement's worldview, such as the need to "protect children" from elite corruption or to "take back" power from unseen forces. These allusions serve as dog whistles, signaling to QAnon supporters without alienating mainstream voters who might not be familiar with the movement.

This alignment isn't just rhetorical; it often comes with practical, grassroots support. QAnon followers, galvanized by their belief in a hidden battle between good and evil, are enthusiastic campaigners, organizing rallies, spreading messages on social media, and creating homemade campaign materials for candidates they believe align with their cause. This organic support provides a grassroots energy that some candidates find irresistible. In primary races, where a dedicated base can make or break a campaign, QAnon supporters can be especially influential. By tapping into this energy, candidates can gain an advantage over opponents, winning support from a base that views political action as part of a larger mission.

Campaign strategies have also evolved to address QAnon's influence, with candidates sometimes subtly adjusting their platforms to cater to or distance themselves from the movement. In districts where QAnon's influence is strong, some candidates have courted followers by promising to investigate the issues QAnon promotes, such as elite corruption or alleged government cover-ups. Conversely, candidates in less QAnon-friendly areas often feel the need to explicitly denounce the movement, walking a fine line between alienating QAnon supporters and losing credibility with moderate voters. For many candidates, navigating QAnon's presence has become a strategic balancing act, as they weigh the benefits of attracting a devoted following against the risks of endorsing a movement with controversial and widely debunked claims.

QAnon's effect on campaign funding has also been notable. Through donations and small-scale fundraising efforts, QAnon followers have financially supported candidates who appear sympathetic to their beliefs. Social media campaigns and crowdfunding platforms have enabled QAnon supporters to rally behind candidates who might otherwise struggle to fund their campaigns. In some cases, QAnon supporters have pooled resources to create significant financial backing, using their collective power to support candidates who they believe will champion their cause. This financial support doesn't only bolster QAnon-aligned candidates; it also signals to other politicians that QAnon's influence is a force worth considering in shaping campaign messages.

The movement's influence has presented unique challenges for mainstream political parties and candidates attempting to counter QAnon's reach. In highly polarized districts, politicians find themselves confronted with a choice: distance themselves from QAnon and risk losing votes from a fervent base, or adopt the movement's language and ideas to appeal to its supporters. This dilemma often leads to uncomfortable choices and contradictory messaging, especially for parties that want to avoid the movement's more radical elements while still appealing to a politically diverse electorate. In this environment, campaigns are forced to contend not only with typical issues like healthcare and jobs but with increasingly polarized, conspiracy-driven narratives that overshadow traditional political discourse.

QAnon's involvement in American elections has thus reshaped campaign strategies, injected unconventional rhetoric into the mainstream, and created new dynamics that blur the lines between grassroots activism and ideological extremism. Candidates who openly or subtly align with QAnon gain access to a passionate, loyal voter base willing to support them financially, promote their platforms, and spread their messages. For those running for office, QAnon's influence offers both an opportunity and a challenge, forcing them to navigate an electorate that is increasingly divided, politically charged, and, in some cases, guided by narratives that go beyond traditional campaign issues. In this transformed landscape, QAnon has left a lasting mark, challenging politicians to consider the movement's role in shaping the future of American electoral politics.

4. Influence on Elected Officials and Policy-Making

As QAnon's influence spread beyond internet forums and entered mainstream politics, it began shaping the decisions and actions of elected officials across the United States. Some officials openly embrace QAnon ideas, seeing the movement as a way to galvanize support among a loyal base. For others, QAnon's impact is more subtle, with followers' concerns pressuring them to address issues that align with QAnon's narrative. This influence has extended into policy discussions, as QAnon-affiliated representatives advocate for legislation inspired by the movement's themes. The presence of QAnon within government has complicated policy-making, introducing elements of conspiracy theory into the legislative process.

Several elected officials have openly endorsed QAnon or made statements suggesting sympathy for the movement. These representatives often incorporate QAnon's language into their messaging, framing themselves as crusaders against corruption or champions for transparency, aligning with QAnon's perception of a world controlled by a secretive elite. For these officials, embracing QAnon serves as a tool to rally and maintain the loyalty of followers who are passionate about uncovering alleged conspiracies and holding elites accountable. In return, QAnon followers see these officials as allies, representatives who will stand up for their beliefs and challenge the establishment. This reciprocal relationship reinforces both the officials' political position and the followers' loyalty to the movement, as both sides see themselves as united in a shared mission.

Even officials who do not openly support QAnon have felt its influence, especially when confronted with vocal constituents who are deeply invested in the movement's beliefs. At town halls, public meetings, and online forums, elected representatives are often asked about QAnon-related topics, such as child trafficking or the "deep state." While these issues are real and important, QAnon reframes them within a conspiratorial context, pressuring officials to address the concerns in ways that validate followers' suspicions. In many cases, representatives are forced to tread carefully, acknowledging the concerns without fully endorsing the narrative. The pressure from QAnon followers creates a tension between public service and the need to navigate a voter base that may believe in highly specific, often debunked theories.

The QAnon movement has also influenced specific policy discussions, particularly around issues like child protection and human trafficking. Although these issues are valid concerns, QAnon's exaggerated claims—such as the existence of elite-run child trafficking rings or widespread pedophilia among politicians—have shaped policy debates. Some QAnon-affiliated officials propose or support legislation based on QAnon's view of these issues, aiming to "expose" or "protect" the vulnerable in ways that resonate with their followers. While well-intentioned, these proposals can distract from effective solutions by framing the problem in ways that do not align with reality, potentially diverting resources from legitimate anti-trafficking initiatives to policies that play into QAnon's conspiratorial narrative.

QAnon's presence in government also influences how policymakers approach federal oversight and government transparency. For many QAnon followers, the idea of an all-powerful "deep state" controlling society has fostered a belief that federal agencies are corrupt and untrustworthy. Representatives aligned with the movement may push for policies aimed at dismantling or reducing the power of federal agencies, promoting reforms that align with the belief that government institutions are operating with hidden agendas. While accountability and oversight are critical aspects of governance, the influence of QAnon has led to calls for reforms based on unproven theories, which complicates efforts to address legitimate concerns about government transparency without promoting conspiracy-fueled agendas.

The presence of QAnon-aligned officials has also posed challenges for other legislators, particularly those who wish to distance themselves from conspiracy theories while maintaining political alliances. QAnon's influence in Congress and state legislatures creates a layer of complexity in policy discussions, with representatives forced to navigate relationships with colleagues who may openly or subtly support the movement. This dynamic has led to rifts within political parties, as officials who reject QAnon find themselves at odds with colleagues whose rhetoric and actions are influenced by the movement's ideas. For many lawmakers, working alongside QAnon-affiliated representatives means balancing legislative goals with the need to counter conspiracy-based narratives in a way that doesn't alienate potential allies or the constituents who support them.

Ultimately, QAnon's impact on elected officials and policy-making has introduced a unique set of challenges to the American political landscape. By promoting ideas that prioritize conspiratorial beliefs over evidence-based policy, QAnon has influenced how representatives communicate with their constituents, approach legislative issues, and work with colleagues. This influence doesn't just affect those directly aligned with the movement; it also shapes the environment in which all policy-making takes place, creating a landscape where conspiracy theories and unsubstantiated narratives can influence real-world decisions and, in turn, the lives of ordinary Americans. As QAnon's influence continues to grow within government, the movement poses ongoing questions about the role of conspiracy theories in shaping the future of American policy.

5. Implications for Democratic Institutions and Governance

The influence of QAnon has raised significant concerns about the stability of democratic institutions in the United States, challenging foundational pillars of governance, from public trust in government agencies to the rule of law. At its core, QAnon promotes a worldview that casts doubt on nearly every democratic institution, from Congress to the judiciary, fueling a distrust that undermines the functioning of representative democracy. For followers, these institutions are often seen not as vehicles for public service but as tools of control wielded by a powerful, secretive cabal. This narrative erodes confidence in the very systems designed to uphold accountability and transparency, creating a growing divide between QAnon believers and the institutions meant to serve them.

The judiciary, which relies on public confidence in its impartiality, has faced challenges from QAnon's influence. Followers often reject judicial rulings or legal proceedings that contradict their beliefs, viewing them as manipulated by the "deep state" or influenced by elite agendas. When QAnon-affiliated defendants face legal action, followers often interpret these cases as political attacks rather than objective applications of the law. This belief fosters a dangerous precedent where legal outcomes are accepted only when they align with the movement's worldview. Over time, this distrust in the judiciary weakens the perception of the courts as fair and independent, contributing to a societal mindset where the rule of law is seen as subjective rather than universal.

QAnon's messaging also promotes skepticism of Congress, labeling representatives and senators as either complicit in a global conspiracy or actively working to suppress the "truth." Many followers believe that members of Congress are either corrupt or unwilling to challenge powerful interests. This perception, fueled by QAnon narratives, has shifted the public's view of lawmakers from elected officials serving the people to pawns in a hidden game. When Congress fails to act on issues that align with QAnon's worldview, followers often see this as evidence of betrayal, further eroding confidence in the legislative process. This sense of disillusionment makes it increasingly difficult for Congress to function as a unifying body, as QAnon followers see compromise or collaboration with the "other side" as part of the problem, deepening political polarization.

The impact on federal agencies has been profound as well. QAnon's narrative portrays agencies like the FBI, CIA, and DOJ as corrupt institutions working to protect elites rather than the public. This view has led to a surge of distrust in federal law enforcement and intelligence agencies, which are cast as enforcers of an anti-democratic agenda rather than as protectors of national security. Followers often believe that these agencies are suppressing evidence or protecting the cabal, leading them to reject investigations, public advisories, and even national security efforts. This erosion of trust undermines the work of these agencies, making it harder to combat threats and enforce laws effectively, as significant segments of the population question the agencies' legitimacy.

Beyond distrust in individual institutions, QAnon's rhetoric has led some followers to embrace anti-democratic ideals, including calls for violent resistance against perceived enemies. The movement's language often frames followers as soldiers in a hidden war, encouraging them to "take action" to expose the cabal. This mindset has incited some QAnon supporters to threaten violence against officials, government buildings, and public figures. The potential for violence has prompted law enforcement to treat QAnon as a domestic terrorism threat, recognizing the danger that comes from a movement that sees political and institutional challenges as a righteous crusade. This atmosphere has created a tense environment for both politicians and citizens, undermining the democratic principle of peaceful discourse and challenging the safety of public officials and institutions.

The long-term implications for American democracy are profound. If public confidence in institutions continues to decline under the influence of conspiracy-driven narratives like QAnon, the country could face a future where significant portions of the population no longer engage with democratic processes or view them as legitimate. Elections, judicial rulings, and legislative actions could lose their authority among QAnon believers, leading to a fractured society where facts, rules, and standards are no longer universally accepted. This erosion of a shared reality makes governing difficult and could lead to a society where separate factions operate with their own "truths," rendering collective decision-making nearly impossible.

In the broader scope of governance, QAnon's influence demonstrates the vulnerability of democratic institutions to disinformation and conspiracy theories. As QAnon's narrative spreads, it forces institutions to grapple with unprecedented challenges, including restoring public trust, countering misinformation, and addressing security risks posed by radicalized followers. The movement's success in undermining democratic institutions serves as a warning of the potential consequences when widespread distrust takes root in society. American democracy, built on the ideals of transparency, accountability, and public engagement, faces a test: to restore trust in institutions and ensure that the principles of governance can withstand the strain of disinformation.

Ultimately, QAnon has revealed the fragility of democratic institutions when public confidence is compromised. For the United States, the road ahead will require a concerted effort to rebuild trust, promote media literacy, and safeguard institutions from the destabilizing effects of conspiracy theories. Without these efforts, the impact of movements like QAnon could continue to reverberate, challenging the very foundation of American democracy and reshaping the relationship between the public and the institutions that serve them.

Chapter 7: The Role of Social Media

1. Viral Spread: How Social Media Accelerated QAnon's Growth

The viral nature of social media was instrumental in transforming QAnon from a fringe conspiracy into a global movement. In the early days, QAnon lived primarily on obscure message boards like 4chan and 8chan, which, though anonymous and unfiltered, had a limited reach. But social media changed the game. Platforms like Facebook, Twitter, Instagram, and YouTube gave QAnon a powerful boost, allowing it to break out of the shadows and reach millions of people with ease. Through the simple act of sharing, QAnon's message spread from user to user, group to group, crossing geographical, cultural, and ideological boundaries almost overnight.

At the heart of this spread were social media features that encouraged rapid sharing and reposting. Each time a QAnon follower shared a Q drop, theory, or meme, it could reach hundreds or even thousands of people within seconds. QAnon followers used hashtags like #WWG1WGA ("Where We Go One, We Go All") and #SaveTheChildren to amplify their content and attract people who might not otherwise engage with conspiracy theories. Hashtags allowed QAnon content to be easily searchable and placed it alongside posts from unrelated movements, helping it attract attention from people who might be sympathetic to its messages. This strategy wasn't accidental; it was a deliberate attempt to spread QAnon's message and draw in new followers who felt they were joining a cause.

Memes played a particularly effective role in making QAnon accessible. Complex, convoluted theories that might have otherwise felt overwhelming were simplified into digestible, compelling memes that were easily shared and understood. These images and short videos packaged the QAnon message in a way that felt engaging and approachable, often using humor, irony, or striking visuals to attract attention. Memes allowed QAnon followers to connect with one another, spreading a shared language and set of symbols that united them under a common banner. The format also allowed followers to sidestep the need for deeper engagement; a meme could convey the essence of a theory without requiring the viewer to read extensive posts or understand the intricate backstory. For a new follower, sharing a meme was an easy entry point into the movement.

The structure of social media itself—the endless scroll, the constant updates, and the accessibility—amplified QAnon's reach. Each platform's design encouraged followers to post frequently, engage with others, and grow their networks, creating a self-sustaining loop of content creation and sharing. QAnon's message thrived in this environment, reaching people who might never have encountered it otherwise. Algorithms that prioritize highly engaging content ensured that QAnon posts gained visibility, especially as followers' enthusiastic engagement boosted their reach. As people liked, shared, and commented on QAnon content, algorithms interpreted these actions as signs of interest, further amplifying the material across feeds and timelines.

As QAnon spread across platforms, it gained momentum, rapidly drawing in followers from all walks of life. Social media allowed the movement to connect like-minded people, creating networks of followers who felt they had discovered something profound, hidden from view. Followers who might have once felt isolated in their beliefs found a community where they could discuss theories, interpret Q drops, and share insights. This shared experience strengthened the movement's cohesion, helping followers feel that they were part of something meaningful, a collective mission to reveal the truth.

Social media's viral capabilities transformed QAnon from a fringe curiosity into a sprawling movement with international reach. The ease of sharing, the appeal of hashtags, the simplicity of memes, and the power of algorithms created the perfect environment for QAnon's message to flourish. What began as a small community on anonymous message boards exploded into a global phenomenon, driven by the very platforms that were designed to connect people across distances. For QAnon, social media didn't just provide a way to communicate; it became the lifeblood of the movement, enabling it to grow beyond anyone's expectations.

2. The Influence of Algorithms: Amplifying Conspiracy Content

Algorithms—those unseen mathematical formulas that decide what content social media users see—played a critical role in QAnon's explosive growth. Platforms like Facebook, YouTube, and Twitter use algorithms to prioritize content that keeps users engaged, promoting posts that garner likes, shares, and comments. For QAnon, these algorithms acted as an inadvertent megaphone, amplifying conspiracy-laden posts to larger and more diverse audiences. As QAnon posts spurred high levels of engagement, the algorithms interpreted this as interest, pushing QAnon content further into people's feeds, even for those who might not have sought it out.

The impact of algorithms on platforms like YouTube was especially profound. YouTube's recommendation system is designed to keep users watching, suggesting videos based on what they've previously viewed. QAnon videos, often lengthy and sensational, tapped directly into this system, drawing viewers deeper into the movement. Users who watched videos on topics related to government distrust, conspiracy theories, or "alternative" news sources found themselves directed toward QAnon content. A viewer might start by watching a video about political scandals, only to be led down a rabbit hole of QAnon-related content without actively searching for it. The algorithm's goal was simple: keep users engaged. But for QAnon, this goal meant pushing followers further into a world of conspiratorial thinking.

Facebook's algorithm also played a pivotal role in QAnon's rise. Designed to show users content similar to what they'd previously engaged with, Facebook's system fed QAnon posts into the news feeds of followers' friends and acquaintances, broadening the reach of each post. QAnon followers who engaged heavily with Q-related content would see more of it, creating an insular environment where conspiracy theories dominated their feeds. Additionally, Facebook's group recommendations, which suggest related communities based on users' interests, introduced new followers to QAnon groups. Once inside, users found themselves in echo chambers where every post, comment, and shared link reinforced the movement's beliefs. The insular nature of these groups turned them into breeding grounds for QAnon's more extreme views, with little outside influence to counterbalance the narratives being shared.

Twitter's algorithmic timeline also contributed to QAnon's visibility. As QAnon-related tweets gained engagement through retweets, likes, and replies, Twitter's algorithm promoted these tweets more broadly, showcasing them to users who followed accounts with similar interests or interacted with related hashtags. Hashtags like #WWG1WGA and #TheGreatAwakening became trendable tools, elevating QAnon content beyond the circle of its immediate followers. Each retweet or like signaled to the algorithm that this was content worth spreading, helping QAnon discussions reach an ever-widening audience and bringing more people into the movement.

This algorithmic amplification created a pipeline from casual interest to deeper involvement in QAnon. Someone might stumble upon a QAnon meme or post through a friend's share, then engage with related content, and soon find themselves immersed in a world of QAnon theories, videos, and groups. The algorithms shaped this journey, guiding users toward increasingly conspiratorial content as they engaged more with each piece of QAnon material. For many followers, what began as mild curiosity quickly became a consuming experience, as the algorithms led them deeper into QAnon's universe with each click and scroll.

The challenge for social media companies became clear as QAnon's influence grew: the very systems designed to maximize engagement were fueling the spread of misinformation. Efforts to counter QAnon's reach through algorithm adjustments, content moderation, and fact-checking proved complex and, in many cases, insufficient. By the time platforms began implementing strategies to reduce QAnon's visibility, the movement had already gained a massive foothold. Algorithms had given QAnon the reach and visibility to transform from a niche conspiracy theory into a global phenomenon, leaving platforms struggling to undo the effects of years of amplified conspiratorial content.

In the end, algorithms amplified QAnon far beyond what any grassroots movement could have achieved on its own. By prioritizing engagement over accuracy, social media algorithms enabled QAnon to thrive in a system that rewarded sensationalism and high interaction. For QAnon, the algorithms were more than just a feature of social media—they were a gateway, ushering in waves of new followers and embedding the movement deep within the social media landscape.

3. The Role of Influencers: Spreading and Validating QAnon Narratives

Influencers were instrumental in QAnon's rise, acting as trusted voices who interpreted and spread Q's cryptic messages to followers. In the early days, QAnon posts were fragmented and cryptic, written in vague terms on message boards, often requiring interpretation to make any sense. This need for "decoders" created a fertile ground for influencers to emerge as leaders within the movement. These influencers, who often built their followings on platforms like YouTube, Twitter, and Instagram, became essential figures, translating Q's posts into a coherent narrative and guiding followers through the complex web of conspiracy theories. For many QAnon followers, these influencers weren't just commentators—they were mentors, trusted voices who brought structure and clarity to the movement.

These QAnon influencers, often self-styled investigators or citizen journalists, created content that drew thousands—and eventually, millions—of viewers. YouTube channels and Twitter accounts dedicated to QAnon grew exponentially as influencers produced videos, livestreams, and threads breaking down each Q drop, explaining connections, and building new theories. Their content took on an educational tone, with influencers presenting themselves as experts in decoding Q's messages and explaining world events through the lens of the conspiracy. Followers saw these influencers as authorities within the movement, voices who could be trusted to interpret the clues and reveal the hidden truths that QAnon promised.

Many influencers monetized their QAnon content, benefiting financially from the movement's growth. Through ads, donations, and subscriber-only content on platforms like Patreon, these influencers capitalized on the enthusiasm of their followers. Some offered exclusive livestreams, early access to new videos, or special forums where followers could discuss theories and ask questions directly. This structure helped influencers sustain and expand their platforms, turning QAnon content into a profitable venture. The promise of insider access or exclusive content also deepened followers' loyalty, making them feel part of an exclusive club and reinforcing the sense that they were on a mission to uncover hidden truths.

The content produced by these influencers did more than just explain QAnon—it provided a structure and narrative framework that kept followers engaged. Influencers would analyze current events, often twisting or cherry-picking information to fit QAnon's themes, linking news headlines, celebrity actions, or government policies back to the movement's core beliefs. For instance, a high-profile arrest or political scandal might be reframed as part of the "storm" QAnon followers believed was coming. In this way, influencers created a continuous storyline, casting world events as chapters in a grand, unfolding plot. This interpretive role gave QAnon followers a consistent and compelling narrative that aligned with their worldview, drawing them deeper into the movement with each new video, post, or livestream.

The role of influencers also extended to providing followers with a sense of community. Many QAnon followers joined these influencers' livestreams, social media groups, or forums, where they could interact with like-minded people. Through comment sections, live chats, and social media posts, followers connected with each other and with the influencers, creating a feedback loop that reinforced their beliefs. Influencers encouraged this participation, often addressing followers by name, answering questions in real-time, and validating their ideas. This interaction strengthened the sense of belonging within the movement, making QAnon feel less like a theory and more like a tightly knit community united by shared beliefs.

In essence, QAnon's influencers did more than interpret and amplify the movement's ideas—they gave QAnon a personal touch, a sense of connection, and a storyline that kept followers captivated. By creating a framework for understanding Q's messages and tying them to real-world events, these influencers transformed QAnon from a fragmented collection of theories into a cohesive narrative. For followers, these influencers were both guides and gatekeepers, validating their beliefs and helping them feel part of something significant. Through their videos, posts, and interactions, QAnon's influencers built a movement that transcended the online world, creating a sense of purpose, belonging, and trust that made QAnon resilient, self-sustaining, and nearly immune to outside criticism.

4. Evasion of Moderation and Platform Policies

As QAnon's influence grew, social media platforms began facing pressure to moderate or ban QAnon-related content. However, QAnon followers proved remarkably adaptive, quickly finding ways to evade detection and circumvent moderation efforts. This ability to sidestep platform policies became a defining feature of the movement, allowing it to maintain its presence online despite increased scrutiny. Followers developed techniques to stay one step ahead, using code words, alternative hashtags, and migrating to fringe platforms when necessary. This evasive strategy not only preserved QAnon's online footprint but also fostered a sense of resilience and ingenuity within the movement.

One of the most common strategies QAnon followers used to evade moderation was code-switching—replacing specific keywords, hashtags, or phrases to avoid detection by automated content filters. For instance, when hashtags like #WWG1WGA or #QAnon began triggering moderation alerts, followers adopted subtle alternatives, such as using initials, symbols, or abbreviations that conveyed the same message without drawing attention. Phrases like "The Great Awakening" or "Save Our Children" replaced explicit QAnon terminology, allowing followers to continue spreading their ideas under a cloak of seemingly innocuous language. This flexibility kept QAnon content flowing on mainstream platforms, making it difficult for moderators to detect and remove it without affecting unrelated discussions.

As platforms like Facebook, Twitter, and YouTube ramped up their efforts to restrict QAnon content, followers began migrating to fringe platforms that offered fewer restrictions. Sites like Parler, Gab, and Telegram became safe havens for QAnon, providing followers with spaces where they could freely share theories, discuss Q drops, and organize without fear of being banned. These platforms became echo chambers, where QAnon content went largely unchecked and followers were surrounded by like-minded individuals. The migration to these alternative networks strengthened the movement's insularity, creating communities that reinforced QAnon's narratives and encouraged deeper belief in the conspiracy. For followers, the shift to fringe platforms wasn't just a practical solution; it was a statement of defiance against what they saw as censorship by mainstream media.

In addition to moving to fringe platforms, QAnon supporters employed techniques to keep their content less conspicuous on mainstream platforms. Followers would post QAnon content under unrelated or trending hashtags, using popular topics to camouflage their posts. By linking QAnon ideas to general political or social issues, they gained access to a broader audience without immediately flagging the attention of moderators. Some even embedded QAnon references in posts about current events, allowing the content to slip under the radar by appearing as commentary on mainstream topics. This approach made it harder for content filters to target QAnon posts directly, as they were woven into wider online discussions.

Moderators struggled to keep up with these evasive tactics, as QAnon's followers continuously adapted their methods. Automated content moderation tools, which often relied on keyword detection, were easily circumvented by QAnon's creative language shifts and use of coded language. Manual moderation, which requires human review, proved insufficient given the sheer volume of QAnon content and the speed at which followers evolved their tactics. The movement's resilience created a cat-and-mouse dynamic between platforms and followers, where each new restriction was met with an equally innovative workaround. This ongoing adaptation only deepened QAnon's followers' belief that they were under attack for uncovering "the truth," reinforcing their commitment to spreading the message despite the barriers.

The effectiveness of these evasive tactics presented social media companies with a dilemma: how to balance the need for moderation with respect for free expression. Platforms faced backlash from both QAnon followers, who saw moderation as censorship, and the public, who demanded accountability for the spread of harmful conspiracy theories. The platforms' inability to contain QAnon's content fueled the movement's growth, allowing it to retain a presence on mainstream social media while fostering robust communities on alternative platforms. In the end, QAnon's adaptability became one of its defining strengths, enabling it to thrive in an environment increasingly hostile to its ideas and underscoring the challenge of controlling misinformation in the digital age.

5. The Ongoing Challenge: Balancing Free Speech and Misinformation Control

The rise of QAnon presented social media platforms with one of their most difficult challenges: how to balance free speech with the need to control the spread of harmful misinformation. QAnon content often blurred the line between political speech and conspiracy theory, creating a gray area that made moderation complicated. Social media companies like Facebook, Twitter, and YouTube found themselves at the center of a debate that weighed the protection of open discourse against the risks posed by disinformation that could incite violence or undermine democratic institutions. The question became not only how to handle QAnon but what responsibility social media platforms have in managing the spread of dangerous ideas.

Initially, many platforms were hesitant to take drastic action against QAnon, citing concerns over freedom of expression. Social media companies have long positioned themselves as neutral spaces for discussion, aiming to provide a forum where users could engage with diverse perspectives. However, as QAnon's influence spread, so did the reports of real-world harm. From followers harassing public figures to threats against government institutions, QAnon began manifesting beyond the digital world, making its containment more urgent. This escalation forced platforms to confront the potential consequences of inaction, prompting a shift in how they approached content moderation for QAnon and other conspiracy theories.

In response, platforms began implementing a range of strategies aimed at curbing QAnon's influence while attempting to uphold free speech. Fact-checking initiatives labeled certain posts as misleading, hoping that users would think twice before believing or sharing questionable content. Some platforms opted to hide or downrank QAnon-related content in search results and newsfeeds, a subtle way of reducing visibility without outright bans. This approach allowed platforms to avoid accusations of censorship while attempting to slow the spread of conspiracy-laden content. However, these methods were only partially effective, as QAnon followers were often already deeply committed and likely to disregard fact-checking labels as "mainstream media bias" or further proof of a cover-up.

As QAnon's reach and potential for harm became increasingly clear, platforms resorted to stronger measures, including bans and account suspensions. In 2020, Twitter, Facebook, and YouTube took significant steps to ban QAnon groups, pages, and accounts associated with spreading conspiracy theories and inciting violence. This move marked a turning point in social media moderation, signaling that platforms were willing to restrict access to certain types of content to protect public safety. For some users, however, these bans were seen as a violation of free speech, sparking a backlash that accused platforms of selectively silencing voices. The response illustrated the delicate balance platforms had to strike: satisfying demands for accountability without alienating users who felt their rights were being infringed.

The ongoing struggle to control QAnon content highlighted the limitations of current moderation tools and strategies. Automated systems could detect certain keywords or phrases, but QAnon followers quickly adapted, using coded language and alternative hashtags to evade detection. This forced platforms to rely on a combination of algorithms and human moderators, a labor-intensive process that was still unable to catch every instance of QAnon content. Moreover, as mainstream platforms cracked down on QAnon, followers migrated to alternative sites like Parler and Gab, where fewer restrictions allowed QAnon communities to flourish unchecked. This migration underscored the difficulty of fully containing the movement within a decentralized online ecosystem.

For social media companies, the challenge of moderating QAnon revealed a broader dilemma in addressing misinformation: how to balance the protection of democratic values with the risks of unchecked conspiracies. Many followers saw the moderation efforts as evidence that they were on the right path, interpreting bans and suspensions as further proof that the establishment was trying to silence them. This paradox illustrated the complexities of moderating belief-driven communities, where efforts to control information could reinforce followers' commitment to their cause rather than dissuade them.

The QAnon experience has reshaped the conversation around social media responsibility, highlighting the need for platforms to develop more nuanced moderation policies that go beyond simple bans or fact-checking labels. It also demonstrated that misinformation can be a resilient, adaptable force, especially when it offers followers a sense of purpose or community. As platforms continue to navigate the balance between free speech and misinformation control, the lessons from QAnon underscore the necessity of proactive, transparent policies that can adapt to the evolving digital landscape. In many ways, QAnon's persistence serves as a cautionary tale, challenging platforms to confront the unique power and dangers of online movements in an era where misinformation can spread as quickly as the click of a button.

Chapter 8: Global Spread of the Theory

1. Factors Driving QAnon's International Spread

QAnon began as a distinctly American conspiracy theory, rooted in U.S. political culture and centered around American institutions. However, within a few years, QAnon's influence crossed borders, spreading to countries around the world. Followers emerged in Europe, Latin America, Asia, and beyond, adapting the theory to fit their own national landscapes. The global spread of QAnon was fueled by several key factors that made it uniquely adaptable and resonant across diverse cultures. Chief among these were the pervasive influence of social media, the impact of the COVID-19 pandemic, the cultural reach of American media, and a shared global disillusionment with governments and elites.

Social media played a crucial role in connecting QAnon followers across continents, creating a network that allowed information to flow seamlessly between borders. Platforms like Facebook, Twitter, YouTube, and Telegram served as conduits, enabling people from vastly different backgrounds to interact, share ideas, and discuss QAnon theories. Hashtags like #WWG1WGA and #SaveTheChildren transcended linguistic barriers, uniting followers who felt alienated by their own national institutions. Through social media, QAnon became a digital community that offered a sense of belonging and purpose to anyone, anywhere, who shared its worldview. This sense of global camaraderie made QAnon more than a localized conspiracy—it became an international movement where followers saw themselves as part of a global mission to uncover hidden truths.

The COVID-19 pandemic further accelerated QAnon's spread by creating a climate of fear, uncertainty, and isolation that fueled conspiracy thinking. With lockdowns and quarantines keeping people indoors, millions turned to the internet to find answers to their anxieties. Misinformation about the virus, public health measures, and vaccines circulated widely, creating fertile ground for conspiracy theories to take root. QAnon's narrative, with its focus on elite manipulation and hidden threats, resonated deeply in this environment. The pandemic's global impact made it a rallying point for people who felt powerless and skeptical of official explanations, drawing many to QAnon as they searched for alternative narratives. In countries around the world, the pandemic became intertwined with QAnon's core beliefs, creating a universal narrative that seemed to validate followers' fears and suspicions.

American media's cultural reach also played a role in making QAnon accessible worldwide. American politics, entertainment, and news are followed globally, shaping perceptions and providing a sense of familiarity with U.S.-centered issues. For people who were already aware of American political figures and institutions, QAnon's narratives were easier to grasp. The imagery of QAnon—the references to child trafficking, "deep state" conspiracies, and the heroic struggle against elites—aligned with tropes that have long been part of popular culture, from movies to television. This familiarity allowed QAnon's message to resonate even among audiences with limited understanding of U.S. politics, as they could quickly connect the movement's ideas with archetypes and themes that felt universally understandable.

A shared disillusionment with governments and elites further bridged the cultural gaps that might have otherwise limited QAnon's spread. Across countries and continents, people harbored similar grievances: frustration with inequality, distrust in political institutions, and anger at perceived corruption. QAnon provided a framework for these concerns, portraying governments and powerful figures as puppeteers controlling society for their own gain. For people who felt unheard or disenfranchised, QAnon offered a narrative that validated their anger, connecting them to a movement that promised to expose hidden injustices and take power back from the elites. This shared frustration created a universal appeal, allowing QAnon's U.S.-centric origins to adapt seamlessly to different national contexts, where followers could reinterpret the conspiracy to fit their local issues and concerns.

Ultimately, QAnon's global spread was enabled by a unique combination of digital connectivity, global crises, cultural resonance, and widespread disillusionment. These factors helped transform QAnon from a niche American conspiracy theory into a borderless movement that adapted to local landscapes while retaining its core messages of distrust and defiance. As the movement grew internationally, it became clear that QAnon had tapped into something much larger than itself—a collective anxiety and frustration that knew no borders, turning a distinctly American phenomenon into a global one.

2. Cultural Adaptation: QAnon's Localization in Different Countries

As QAnon spread across borders, it underwent a process of cultural adaptation that allowed its message to resonate within diverse national contexts. While the movement's central ideas remained the same—an alleged cabal of elites secretly controlling society for sinister purposes—followers in different countries reinterpreted these ideas to reflect their own unique political climates, cultural concerns, and historical grievances. This localization was crucial to QAnon's international success, as it allowed the theory to feel relevant and immediate, even when its original U.S.-centric details did not apply. By blending its core narrative with local issues and symbols, QAnon adapted to fit seamlessly into different societies, creating a global but culturally diverse phenomenon.

In Germany, for example, QAnon followers incorporated elements of long-standing distrust in the government and concerns over authoritarianism. German QAnon groups quickly adopted narratives linking QAnon's "deep state" with perceived abuses by German politicians and global organizations like the European Union. The movement merged with pre-existing right-wing sentiments and drew connections between QAnon's message and Germany's history of anti-establishment thought, particularly among groups skeptical of both government power and globalization. By aligning QAnon's narrative with Germany's concerns over sovereignty and freedom, followers created a version of the theory that resonated on a national level, making it feel less like an American import and more like a homegrown movement against perceived threats to German identity and autonomy.

In the United Kingdom, QAnon adapted to align with domestic issues such as Brexit, government mistrust, and dissatisfaction with public institutions. British followers found that QAnon's messages about elites and corruption fit neatly into existing grievances surrounding political dysfunction and economic inequality. QAnon gained traction among individuals disillusioned by years of political upheaval and skepticism toward leaders in both major parties. For many, QAnon offered an explanation for the UK's political challenges, framing them as the result of elite manipulation. By incorporating references to British political figures and institutions, QAnon followers in the UK were able to shape the theory into a narrative that addressed their own concerns, making the movement feel relevant to their national situation.

In France, QAnon merged with long-standing sentiments of distrust in authority and anti-elitism, particularly among the "yellow vest" protesters who had already taken to the streets in opposition to perceived economic and social injustices. QAnon's narrative of a corrupt elite pulling society's strings appealed to French citizens who felt marginalized and betrayed by their government. Many saw parallels between QAnon's call to expose the "deep state" and their own frustration with government policies they viewed as favoring the wealthy. French QAnon groups began connecting the movement's themes with national issues like pension reform, police conduct, and labor rights. This adaptation allowed QAnon to tap into France's tradition of populist and anti-establishment movements, making it feel like a continuation of a long-standing fight against entrenched power.

In South America, QAnon's message also found fertile ground, particularly among communities where distrust of government institutions was already high. In countries like Brazil and Argentina, QAnon followers wove the theory into narratives about corruption and inequality, adapting it to reflect local political dynamics. Brazilian QAnon followers, for instance, connected the movement's themes to their own political battles, framing the "deep state" as a global network that influenced local issues like crime, corruption, and economic instability. This version of QAnon capitalized on Brazil's political polarization, with supporters linking the movement's ideas to perceived threats against their own government's sovereignty and to accusations of interference by international organizations. In this way, QAnon in South America came to embody a broader narrative about national resilience against external forces.

QAnon's adaptability to different cultures and contexts speaks to the movement's ideological flexibility. Its core themes—distrust of elites, belief in hidden threats, and a commitment to exposing the truth—could be molded to fit almost any political climate. The movement's followers didn't need to believe every detail of the American version; they could reinterpret the theory to focus on their own elites, authorities, and institutions. This allowed QAnon to transcend its original form, reshaping itself to fit the concerns and fears of people in vastly different regions. As a result, QAnon became not just an American conspiracy theory, but a global framework for interpreting political and social discontent, resonating in culturally specific ways across the world.

3: State and Local Payroll Taxes

Beyond federal payroll taxes, businesses must also navigate a range of state and local payroll taxes, which can vary significantly based on the business's location. State and local taxes often include income tax withholding, unemployment insurance, disability insurance, and other region-specific requirements. This section will cover the different types of state and local taxes businesses may encounter, along with strategies for managing compliance efficiently. Staying informed about these tax requirements is crucial, as penalties for noncompliance can be substantial.

State Income Tax Withholding

One of the most common types of state payroll tax is income tax withholding. While not all states impose an income tax, the majority do, and each has its own tax rates, withholding requirements, and filing schedules. States like Florida and Texas, for instance, have no state income tax, whereas others, such as California and New York, have progressive tax rates based on income levels. To ensure compliance, employers must withhold the correct amount based on each employee's earnings and file these amounts with the state's revenue agency.

Each state has its own withholding guidelines, and employees are usually required to submit a state-specific withholding certificate—similar to the federal W-4—to determine how much should be withheld from their paychecks. Some states also offer reciprocal tax agreements with neighboring states. These agreements allow employees who live in one state but work in another to pay income tax only to their state of residence, simplifying withholding for employers. Understanding state-specific regulations and staying up-to-date with tax rate changes is critical to managing state income tax accurately.

State Unemployment Insurance (SUI)

State Unemployment Insurance (SUI) is a tax that employers pay to fund unemployment benefits for eligible workers. SUI rates and wage bases vary widely by state, and these taxes are typically based on the employer's experience rating, which reflects their history of unemployment claims. A lower experience rating—indicating fewer claims—can reduce the employer's SUI rate, potentially leading to significant cost savings.

Each state has its own requirements for SUI contributions, including different wage bases and rates that are adjusted annually. Employers are responsible for monitoring changes in their experience rating and understanding how it impacts their SUI obligations. Some states require both employers and employees to contribute to unemployment insurance, though in most cases, only employers are liable. Regularly reviewing SUI obligations and leveraging any tax credits available through timely and complete payments is essential for effective payroll management.

Disability Insurance Requirements

In addition to income and unemployment taxes, some states mandate disability insurance (DI) contributions to support workers who become temporarily disabled due to illness or injury unrelated to their jobs. States with DI requirements include California, New York, New Jersey, Hawaii, and Rhode Island. The specifics of DI programs vary, but in most cases, both employers and employees contribute to these funds.

Disability insurance is generally calculated as a small percentage of the employee's gross wages and may have a maximum annual contribution limit. DI rates and requirements can change annually, and employers are required to withhold the correct amount from employees' wages and remit it to the state's disability insurance program. Understanding the DI requirements in your state and ensuring accurate contributions help ensure compliance and provide employees with essential benefits.

Local Payroll Taxes

In addition to state taxes, certain cities and counties impose local payroll taxes. Local taxes are often levied to support municipal services like public transportation, infrastructure, and schools. These taxes can vary considerably by location and may apply only to residents or individuals who work within specific city or county boundaries. For example, cities like Philadelphia and San Francisco impose payroll taxes on employees or employers, while New York City has its own set of income tax rates for residents.

Local payroll taxes may be based on a percentage of gross wages or a flat amount per employee, depending on the jurisdiction. Employers are responsible for understanding and adhering to local tax requirements in the areas where their employees work and reside. Payroll software with geolocation features can be helpful for businesses with employees in multiple locations, as it can automatically calculate and apply the correct local tax rates based on each employee's work address.

Managing Compliance Across Multiple Jurisdictions

For employers operating in multiple states or regions, managing compliance for various payroll taxes can be complex. However, there are several strategies to simplify the process:

1. **Centralized Payroll Software**: Using a payroll system that integrates federal, state, and local tax requirements is essential for maintaining accuracy. Many payroll software solutions automatically update tax rates and regulations, making it easier to stay compliant across jurisdictions.

2. **Stay Informed on Regulatory Changes**: Tax laws are subject to change, and states often adjust their rates, wage bases, and filing schedules. Subscribe to updates from relevant state and local tax agencies to stay informed and make timely adjustments to payroll.

3. **Hire a Payroll Specialist**: For larger businesses or those with complex payroll needs, hiring a payroll specialist or partnering with a payroll provider can help ensure compliance across multiple jurisdictions. Payroll specialists are trained to navigate the nuances of state and local taxes, reducing the risk of errors.

4. **Establish Clear Record-Keeping**: Accurate record-keeping is crucial for compliance. Maintain organized records of all payroll tax filings, rates, and remittances for each state and local jurisdiction. These records are essential in case of audits and for internal reviews of payroll processes.

5. **Leverage Geolocation Features in Payroll Systems**: Many modern payroll systems include geolocation tracking, which can automatically assign the correct local tax rates based on

each employee's work location. This is especially useful for businesses with remote or multi-state employees.

Maintaining compliance with state and local payroll taxes requires diligence, organization, and an understanding of the nuances across jurisdictions. While the complexities of these taxes can be challenging, following best practices and staying proactive about regulatory changes can ensure smooth, compliant payroll operations.

Conclusion

State and local payroll taxes, though complex, are integral to a business's payroll responsibilities. By understanding state income taxes, unemployment insurance, disability insurance, and local tax obligations, employers can create a streamlined process that minimizes the risk of penalties. Staying compliant with each jurisdiction's specific requirements is essential, especially as tax rates and regulations change frequently. With the right tools, resources, and strategies, businesses can effectively manage these obligations and support their employees with reliable and accurate payroll.

4. Government and Institutional Responses to QAnon's Global Influence

As QAnon's reach expanded across the globe, governments, law enforcement agencies, and other institutions faced the challenge of addressing the movement's growing influence and the real-world consequences it posed. QAnon's narratives, which often incite distrust toward governments and institutions, placed pressure on authorities to respond proactively, especially as the movement began to inspire acts of extremism, harassment, and violence. From public awareness campaigns to social media regulations, governments worldwide have taken varied approaches to counter QAnon's spread, reflecting the complexity of balancing free speech with public safety in an age of pervasive misinformation.

In Germany, the government took a strong stance against QAnon as it grew popular among far-right groups and anti-lockdown protesters. Law enforcement and intelligence agencies increased surveillance on groups suspected of harboring QAnon supporters, especially as extremist acts linked to the movement raised concerns about potential threats to public order. In some cases, German authorities flagged QAnon followers as potential domestic terrorism risks, citing instances where followers had coordinated online to disrupt public events or confront officials. German officials also launched public awareness campaigns, focusing on educating citizens about the dangers of conspiracy theories and providing tools to help people recognize and debunk misinformation. These campaigns highlighted the psychological techniques used in conspiratorial thinking, equipping the public to critically assess QAnon's claims.

France adopted a similar approach, but with an emphasis on countering misinformation through public education and digital literacy. French authorities worked with social media platforms to restrict QAnon-related content and promote fact-checking initiatives, encouraging users to verify information before sharing. Some French officials have voiced concerns that QAnon, with its anti-elite themes, could fuel existing anti-government sentiments that already resonate among certain segments of the population. To address this, the French government began working with community organizations and schools, aiming to build resilience against conspiracy theories through media literacy programs. By targeting younger generations, France hopes to create a culture of critical thinking that can counteract the appeal of conspiracy movements like QAnon.

In Australia, QAnon has also gained traction, with particular growth during the COVID-19 pandemic as lockdowns fueled suspicion and dissatisfaction with government policies. The Australian government responded by increasing collaboration with social media companies, pushing for more rigorous content moderation to prevent the spread of misinformation. Additionally, Australia has adopted strict penalties for those spreading harmful misinformation related to public health, which has been effective in curbing the circulation of COVID-19-related QAnon theories. Recognizing the mental health impact of QAnon on families, Australian non-profit organizations and mental health services have developed support networks for individuals affected by conspiracy beliefs, offering resources for families to navigate conversations with loved ones who may be deeply involved in QAnon.

The United Kingdom, meanwhile, has approached QAnon's spread by leveraging law enforcement and counter-terrorism units to monitor extremist activity tied to the movement. With the rise of QAnon-linked demonstrations and harassment of public figures, British authorities have taken steps to flag and track individuals who may pose a threat. In response to the social disruption caused by conspiracy theories, the UK has strengthened its digital misinformation strategies, supporting online campaigns to counter QAnon's narrative and working with tech companies to remove harmful content. British officials have acknowledged the difficulty of balancing freedom of expression with the need to prevent online radicalization, recognizing that outright bans may only drive followers to more insular, unregulated platforms.

In the United States, where QAnon originated, the federal government has approached the movement with heightened urgency, particularly following instances of QAnon-linked violence and involvement in the January 6th Capitol riot. The FBI labeled QAnon as a potential domestic terrorism threat, leading to closer monitoring of QAnon-related activities. Government officials and intelligence agencies have actively coordinated with social media platforms to contain QAnon's reach, though this has proven challenging given the movement's adaptability. Additionally, U.S. policymakers have focused on strengthening digital literacy and cybersecurity initiatives to build resilience against misinformation, working with educational institutions to prepare citizens for navigating online disinformation.

The varied responses of governments worldwide reflect the complexity of addressing QAnon's global spread, each country adapting its strategies to fit its unique cultural and political landscape. These responses underscore a common understanding: QAnon represents more than just a conspiracy theory—it's a destabilizing force capable of undermining public trust, encouraging division, and even inciting violence. For governments, addressing QAnon is about protecting public safety and promoting societal cohesion in the face of an online movement that challenges traditional authority structures.

Despite these efforts, QAnon's influence continues to pose significant challenges for institutions worldwide. The movement's adaptability, its use of coded language, and its migration to less regulated platforms make it difficult to fully contain. Governments and institutions face a delicate balancing act: they must protect public safety without infringing on freedom of expression, address misinformation without fueling followers' belief that they are being persecuted, and curb QAnon's spread without driving it further underground. For now, the international response to QAnon remains a patchwork of measures, as governments continue to adapt to an ever-evolving movement that is reshaping how societies think about truth, authority, and the power of belief.

5. Implications of QAnon's Global Spread for International Relations and Society

The global spread of QAnon has had significant implications for international relations, social cohesion, and the stability of democratic institutions worldwide. As the movement has transcended borders, its influence has extended beyond individual followers, affecting the ways countries interact and altering the fabric of societies around the world. The implications of QAnon's rise go beyond the immediate consequences of misinformation; they raise deeper concerns about the ability of democratic societies to withstand the erosion of public trust, the power of digital movements to disrupt international relations, and the potential for an "internationalized" conspiracy culture that unites disparate anti-establishment groups.

One of the most immediate impacts of QAnon's spread has been the strain it places on diplomatic relations. QAnon's narrative often portrays international institutions like the United Nations and the World Health Organization as part of a global conspiracy, which has led to increased skepticism and even hostility toward these organizations. This distrust has complicated cooperation on global issues, as QAnon followers view international initiatives, such as those addressing climate change or public health, with suspicion. The belief that global institutions are corrupt or working against the public interest hampers the ability of nations to come together on shared concerns, creating friction in international collaboration and undermining efforts to address pressing global challenges.

QAnon's influence has also contributed to the erosion of trust in multilateral organizations that rely on the credibility and support of member nations. As QAnon's message spreads, particularly in countries where populist sentiment is already strong, it encourages followers to view their own governments as complicit in a broader international agenda. This has weakened public support for organizations like the European Union in Europe and the WHO globally, as QAnon followers see these entities as orchestrators of globalist agendas that threaten national sovereignty. For many citizens, QAnon's rhetoric has planted seeds of doubt about whether these organizations serve their interests or merely represent the interests of an unseen elite, thereby challenging the foundational trust necessary for multilateral governance.

The spread of QAnon has also fostered an internationalized conspiracy culture that unites groups and individuals across national borders. Followers from different countries find common ground in a shared distrust of elites and a belief in hidden agendas, linking their respective struggles into a broader narrative of global resistance. This "unified" conspiracy mindset has encouraged cooperation among far-right and anti-establishment groups across borders, creating new networks of influence and activism. In Europe, for instance, QAnon has brought together disparate movements that were once focused on national issues, fostering a cross-border conspiracy culture that aligns under the banner of anti-globalism. The result is a more interconnected and potentially volatile international landscape, where conspiracy theories transcend political and cultural boundaries to create a shared, anti-establishment worldview.

The social implications of QAnon's spread are equally profound, as the movement challenges the traditional means by which societies understand truth and authority. With QAnon, followers are encouraged to "do their own research" and seek answers outside of mainstream channels, eroding confidence in established sources of information. This shift has weakened the credibility of journalism, scientific research, and government transparency efforts, as followers reject conventional fact-checking in favor of QAnon's narrative. This mistrust in public institutions and expertise undermines the social contract that holds democratic societies together, as people become less willing to accept information that doesn't align with their beliefs. Over time, this erosion of trust could lead to a fragmented society where shared truths are few and far between, making it increasingly difficult to foster unity, cooperation, and informed public discourse.

Perhaps the most troubling implication of QAnon's global reach is the movement's potential to fuel radicalization and extremism on an international scale. As seen in various countries, QAnon followers have participated in anti-government protests, confronted officials, and even engaged in violent acts inspired by their belief in QAnon's apocalyptic narratives. This radicalization doesn't stop at national borders; rather, QAnon's global spread means that individuals from different countries can come together to reinforce each other's beliefs, share tactics, and encourage actions that challenge governmental authority. The possibility of coordinated, international radicalization poses a serious threat to global security, as individuals who see themselves as part of a worldwide struggle may be more likely to engage in actions that have real-world consequences.

In the long term, the global spread of QAnon highlights the challenge of re-establishing public trust in institutions, especially as societies become increasingly digital and interconnected. Rebuilding this trust will require concerted efforts by governments, media organizations, educational institutions, and tech companies, all of which must work to address the root causes of conspiracy-driven disillusionment. Public education and digital literacy initiatives may help equip people with the tools to critically evaluate online information, but reversing the impact of QAnon will require a broader cultural shift toward valuing truth, transparency, and collective understanding.

QAnon's international growth serves as a warning of the destabilizing power of conspiracy theories in a connected world. It is a reminder of the delicate balance between freedom of expression and the need to protect democratic societies from disinformation that undermines their core principles. As QAnon continues to evolve, the challenges it presents will persist, pushing countries to adapt and find ways to protect the integrity of public discourse. Only by addressing these challenges with a combination of vigilance, resilience, and collaboration can the global community hope to counter the divisive impact of QAnon and prevent similar movements from reshaping the world in the future.

Chapter 9: The Cost of Conspiracy: Families and Co

1. Families Torn Apart: The Emotional and Psychological Toll

QAnon's influence has reached deeply into family life, creating fractures that are often painful and difficult to repair. Families across the globe have found themselves divided by a movement that has reshaped beliefs, values, and priorities for many of its followers. As loved ones become increasingly immersed in QAnon, family dynamics begin to shift, often leading to strained relationships and, in some cases, complete estrangement. The emotional toll is profound; both followers and their families experience intense feelings of frustration, sadness, and helplessness as they struggle to bridge a widening gap that ideology and conspiracy have carved between them.

For many families, the journey starts subtly. A loved one might begin by sharing a few conspiracy-related articles or expressing vague distrust toward institutions. But over time, these views intensify. Conversations that once centered around shared interests and daily events begin to revolve around QAnon theories, with followers passionately advocating for ideas that may sound incomprehensible or frightening to those around them. Family members often find them-selves caught off-guard, unsure how to respond when their loved one begins discussing topics like hidden cabals or elite trafficking rings as if they were established facts. What might start as polite attempts to listen or understand quickly devolves into heated arguments, leaving both sides feeling misunderstood and alienated.

The emotional impact on families can be overwhelming. Parents, siblings, and spouses who once felt close to their loved one may now feel as though they're interacting with a stranger. The person they knew seems distant, often unreceptive to reason, and increasingly defensive. For the loved ones left behind, this transformation can bring about feelings of loss similar to grief, as they grapple with the idea that someone they care about is seemingly lost to a belief system they cannot penetrate. The isolation of losing a loved one to con-spiracy beliefs is compounded by the frustration of feeling powerless to change their perspective. Efforts to reconnect or encourage skep-ticism often backfire, as followers interpret family members' objec-tions as signs that they're "asleep" or part of the problem.

Family gatherings, once a source of joy and unity, often become battlegrounds, where discussions about QAnon erupt into argu-ments that leave everyone feeling wounded. Holidays, birthdays, and celebrations—times meant for connection and joy—can feel tense, as relatives carefully avoid or tiptoe around sensitive topics, hoping to avoid confrontation. In some cases, families find it impossible to continue these gatherings, fearing the inevitable disagreements that will overshadow the occasion. Over time, some families experience estrangement, choosing to avoid contact with loved ones whose be-liefs have become too disruptive. For many, this decision is heart-breaking, but they find it necessary for their own mental and emotional well-being.

QAnon's influence doesn't just affect the individual followers but permeates the entire family, altering relationships and creating ongoing tension. The psychological toll is heavy, with family members often feeling a profound sense of guilt and confusion. They wonder if they could have done something differently or if they missed warning signs along the way. Parents question if they failed to instill critical thinking, while spouses struggle with the reality of sharing a life with someone whose beliefs they no longer understand. The weight of these thoughts adds to the emotional burden, creating a pervasive sense of helplessness that affects family cohesion and individual well-being.

Ultimately, QAnon's impact on families goes beyond mere disagreement; it challenges the very foundation of relationships built on shared values and trust. As family members attempt to navigate this new reality, they face a difficult choice: find a way to maintain a connection with their loved one or, in some cases, accept the painful reality that they may need to distance themselves to protect their own mental health. The emotional and psychological toll of QAnon is not just a byproduct of its beliefs—it is one of the most devastating costs, felt deeply by families who must contend with the loss of connection, understanding, and, in many cases, hope for reconciliation.

2. Friendships and Social Circles: Alienation and Isolation

The spread of QAnon has affected not only family relationships but also friendships and social circles, leading to significant alienation for both followers and those around them. Many friendships that once thrived on shared interests, mutual support, and understanding have been tested—and sometimes broken—by the intensity of QAnon's beliefs. As followers become more deeply immersed in the movement, they often struggle to maintain connections with friends who don't share their perspective, resulting in social isolation that further entrenches them in their newfound worldview.

For many followers, friendships begin to shift as they increasingly bring up QAnon theories in conversations, convinced that sharing their beliefs is a way of "enlightening" those around them. Discussions that once centered on shared hobbies, personal experiences, or everyday topics become dominated by conspiratorial narratives about hidden elites, government control, and secret agendas. Friends who are unfamiliar with or skeptical of QAnon often feel uncomfortable or confused, unsure of how to respond. Initially, some may attempt to humor their friend, hoping it's a phase or that they can offer perspective. But as these conversations persist, friends often find themselves feeling distanced from someone they once knew well, struggling to recognize the person who seems to view every event through a lens of suspicion.

This shift can be particularly painful for long-standing friendships. Friends who have shared memories, milestones, and meaningful experiences may feel a profound sense of loss as they witness a loved one's transformation. They may try to engage in dialogue, hoping to encourage critical thinking or gently challenge some of the more extreme beliefs. However, these attempts are often met with defensiveness, as QAnon followers see questioning as evidence of "closed-mindedness" or complicity in the very system they oppose. Over time, the tension mounts, and many friends find themselves choosing between avoiding certain topics entirely or distancing themselves from the friendship altogether.

The social isolation that follows can be intense, impacting both QAnon followers and those who feel compelled to step away from the relationship. For QAnon believers, losing friends can reinforce their sense of being "awake" in a world that remains "asleep," creating a sense of martyrdom that aligns with the movement's narrative of being misunderstood and opposed by society. As they lose connections with friends who don't share their beliefs, many followers turn to QAnon communities online, finding camaraderie and validation in spaces where their ideas are echoed rather than questioned. These online connections offer a form of social support, but they also create an echo chamber that further isolates followers from differing viewpoints, reinforcing and radicalizing their beliefs.

For friends who step away, the isolation is often tinged with sadness, frustration, and a sense of helplessness. Many struggle with guilt, wondering if there was something more they could have done to reach out or intervene. They may feel a sense of loss for the friendship that once was, left mourning a connection that feels irreparably changed by a force beyond their control. The decision to step back is rarely easy, and many grapple with the decision, feeling torn between loyalty to a friend and the emotional toll of engaging in a relationship that has become draining or divisive.

As QAnon reshapes friendships, it also affects broader social circles, influencing group dynamics in communities, workplaces, and social clubs. Friends who have mutual connections with a QAnon follower may feel pressured to "choose sides" or may avoid gatherings altogether to prevent confrontations. Social circles become fractured, with some friends distancing themselves while others may remain loyal, even if they don't share the follower's beliefs. This division creates a ripple effect, spreading tension and unease across groups that once shared unity and mutual respect.

In the end, QAnon's impact on friendships is profound, leading to a cycle of alienation and isolation that affects both followers and those who care about them. The loss of friendships leaves followers increasingly dependent on QAnon communities for social support, reinforcing their beliefs and creating a sense of belonging that makes it even harder to let go. For those who walk away, the decision is often painful, marked by the loss of connection with someone they once valued deeply. The damage to friendships and social circles highlights one of QAnon's most enduring costs: the way it divides people, creating emotional and social rifts that linger long after the initial belief has taken hold.

3. The Role of Online Communities: Support and Radicalization

Online communities have been both a lifeline and a trap for many QAnon followers. As family and friends grow increasingly distant, QAnon followers turn to online groups for the support, camaraderie, and understanding they no longer find in their offline lives. In these spaces, they are surrounded by like-minded individuals who validate their beliefs, amplify their fears, and provide a sense of belonging that reinforces their commitment to QAnon. These communities foster loyalty and deepen convictions, creating an environment where followers feel seen, heard, and united under a shared mission. However, the same spaces that offer support also function as echo chambers, intensifying followers' beliefs and often pushing them toward more extreme ideologies.

Social media platforms, message boards, and private chat groups serve as hubs where QAnon followers can interact freely. Within these spaces, they find an endless stream of content—videos, memes, articles, and Q drops—that reinforce the movement's narrative. Here, followers are encouraged to "do their own research," digging deeper into conspiracy theories and sharing their "findings" with the community. This practice, which is highly encouraged by group leaders and influencers, fosters a sense of discovery and intellectual independence, even as it further isolates followers from conventional sources of information. Followers become researchers, convinced that they are uncovering hidden truths, which strengthens their loyalty to both QAnon and the online communities that support them.

The echo chamber effect within these online communities is profound. Members reinforce one another's beliefs, rarely encountering dissenting voices or alternative viewpoints. When new ideas or theories are introduced, they are immediately accepted and expanded upon, with little to no critical examination. This dynamic creates an environment where even the most outlandish ideas gain traction and followers become increasingly radicalized. In the absence of external perspectives, the community's collective beliefs grow more extreme, and the shared commitment to "uncovering the truth" becomes an all-consuming mission. Followers who might once have been casual observers of QAnon find themselves drawn deeper into its narratives, motivated by the validation and support they receive from their peers.

Influencers and group leaders within these communities play a critical role in shaping followers' beliefs and actions. Many QAnon influencers present themselves as interpreters of Q drops or as experts who can connect seemingly unrelated events to the movement's larger narrative. Their authority is rarely questioned, and their posts serve as guiding lights for the community, directing followers toward new theories or "evidence" that further entrenches their commitment. These influencers often monetize their content through donations or exclusive subscriber channels, creating a symbiotic relationship where they provide followers with information in exchange for loyalty and financial support. This dynamic not only reinforces the power structure within QAnon communities but also incentivizes influencers to push more sensational, polarizing content that keeps followers engaged.

The support followers find in online communities often comes at the expense of their offline relationships. As they become more invested in QAnon, followers increasingly withdraw from friends and family, viewing anyone outside the movement as part of the "asleep" majority who are either complicit or brainwashed by mainstream narratives. The online community becomes their primary social circle, a space where they can express their beliefs without fear of judgment or criticism. This shift not only deepens their isolation but also strengthens their dependency on QAnon communities, making it harder for them to disengage. For many followers, leaving these communities feels like a betrayal, not only of the movement but also of the friendships and sense of belonging they have cultivated.

The radicalizing effect of QAnon's online communities highlights the dual nature of these spaces: they offer a sense of purpose and community while pulling followers further away from their previous lives. Followers find support, validation, and meaning within these groups, but this comfort comes at the cost of increased isolation and radicalization. The longer followers remain in these communities, the more deeply they internalize QAnon's worldview, making it increasingly difficult for them to break free. In many cases, these communities become the cornerstone of their social identity, replacing offline relationships with a network of like-minded believers bound by a shared sense of mission and distrust of the outside world. For followers, these online spaces are not just support systems—they are worlds of their own, places where they feel fully understood, even as they drift further from the lives they once knew.

4. The Challenge of Intervention: Support Systems and Counseling

For families and friends of QAnon followers, intervening to help a loved one break free from the movement can be an overwhelming and emotionally draining process. Watching someone they care about become increasingly absorbed by QAnon's worldview is painful, and many struggle to find a way to help without alienating their loved one. The challenge lies in approaching followers in a way that respects their autonomy while gently encouraging them to question the beliefs that have isolated them from family, friends, and reality. This process often requires a combination of patience, empathy, and professional support, as the path to disengagement is rarely straightforward.

One of the greatest obstacles to intervention is the defensive posture many QAnon followers adopt. Followers are often deeply distrustful of anyone who questions their beliefs, interpreting skepticism as evidence that others are "brainwashed" or complicit in the very systems they believe they are fighting against. For family members, this reaction can be disheartening, as even well-meaning conversations can spiral into arguments that push the follower further away. Recognizing this defensive mindset, mental health professionals advise that loved ones approach followers with open-ended questions and non-judgmental curiosity, creating space for conversation without forcing a particular perspective. By asking questions rather than making assertions, loved ones can encourage self-reflection, helping followers to gently question the contradictions within QAnon's narratives.

Support systems, both online and in-person, have emerged to assist families navigating these complex situations. Organizations dedicated to countering extremism and conspiracy theories offer resources, such as guides on how to talk to someone who is deeply entrenched in QAnon and support groups for those dealing with similar challenges. These groups provide family members with strategies for communicating effectively, helping them to set realistic expectations and prioritize their own mental health during this challenging process. Many families find solace in these networks, sharing experiences and learning from others who have successfully helped loved ones disengage, finding strength in a community that understands the emotional toll of confronting a loved one's radicalization.

In some cases, counseling or de-radicalization specialists play a crucial role in helping followers reconsider their beliefs. Therapists trained in treating individuals drawn to conspiracy theories approach their work with compassion, aiming to understand the underlying needs that QAnon fulfills for their clients. They often focus on building trust, working to understand what aspects of QAnon resonate most deeply with the follower. For some, QAnon fills a need for purpose, for belonging, or for a sense of control over a confusing world. By addressing these needs and providing alternative ways to find purpose or meaning, therapists can help followers to reconnect with the real world and develop healthier coping mechanisms. This therapeutic approach is delicate and requires sensitivity, as confronting someone directly with facts that challenge their beliefs can backfire, reinforcing their attachment to QAnon's narratives.

In addition to professional help, family members are often encouraged to re-establish connections based on shared values and experiences, rather than trying to dismantle QAnon beliefs head-on. Simple acts, such as revisiting shared memories, engaging in activities that don't touch on conspiracy topics, and showing unconditional support, can remind followers of the relationships they risk losing. By focusing on positive interactions and keeping communication open, families can create a foundation of trust that allows followers to feel secure enough to question their own beliefs gradually. In this way, connection serves as a bridge back to reality, offering a path to self-reflection without the confrontation that often drives followers deeper into the movement.

However, intervention is not always successful, and families often face the heart-wrenching reality that they cannot control their loved one's beliefs. For many, the process of trying to help a loved one break free from QAnon is a long, emotional journey marked by setbacks and, sometimes, permanent estrangement. Recognizing this, mental health professionals encourage family members to take care of their own well-being, setting boundaries when necessary to protect themselves from the psychological strain. While helping a loved one disengage from QAnon can be incredibly rewarding, it is also demanding, and families must balance their desire to support with the need to safeguard their own mental health.

In the end, intervening to help a QAnon follower requires a nuanced approach, one that combines patience, empathy, and professional guidance. The process is rarely quick or straightforward, as deeply held beliefs can be difficult to unravel. But with support systems, counseling, and a commitment to maintaining open, non-judgmental communication, families can play a powerful role in guiding their loved ones back to reality. For those who succeed, the journey is one of resilience, understanding, and healing, as families and friends work together to rebuild trust and reforge connections strained by the grip of QAnon.

5. Long-Term Social Consequences: Divided Communities and Loss of Trust

The impact of QAnon extends far beyond individual followers and their families, leaving long-term scars on communities and society as a whole. As QAnon's ideology has spread, it has created divisions not only between individuals but also within neighborhoods, workplaces, schools, and religious groups. These divisions contribute to a deepening sense of distrust and social fragmentation that persists even as some followers begin to disengage from the movement. The long-term consequences of QAnon are particularly troubling, as the movement has introduced lasting rifts in communities and eroded the social trust that underpins a healthy, functioning society.

In many communities, QAnon has led to a polarization that disrupts social harmony. Neighbors who once exchanged pleasantries now view one another with suspicion, especially in areas where QAnon beliefs are common. Parents, for example, may find themselves at odds over issues like public health policies or educational content, as QAnon narratives about government control and manipulation become flashpoints for local conflict. These disputes extend into school boards, where discussions about curriculum choices or safety protocols can become battlegrounds for QAnon-inspired arguments. Teachers, administrators, and even students can find themselves caught in these ideological crossfires, as conspiracy-fueled distrust disrupts what were once non-partisan, community-focused discussions.

The breakdown of trust also affects local governance. Community leaders, who are typically seen as advocates for public welfare, may find themselves targeted by QAnon followers who view them as part of a corrupt system. In some cases, QAnon adherents have run for local office on platforms that explicitly reflect conspiracy-based beliefs, leading to campaigns that prioritize divisive, unfounded claims over practical solutions to community issues. This shift in local politics can create an environment where public servants are viewed with suspicion, hindering their ability to make decisions that serve the common good. For communities already grappling with issues like economic strain or resource shortages, the presence of QAnon-fueled distrust only exacerbates challenges, making it difficult to rally around collective solutions.

Religious institutions, often a bedrock of community life, have also felt the effects of QAnon. Many followers have woven QAnon's apocalyptic narratives into their spiritual beliefs, creating divisions within congregations. Some church leaders have embraced QAnon's rhetoric, while others have tried to distance their congregations from it, leading to rifts among members who disagree on the movement's place in their faith communities. For congregations, the presence of QAnon can shift the focus from shared religious teachings to divisive conspiracy theories, straining relationships within the faith community. This divide has a lasting impact on the cohesion of religious institutions, which play a crucial role in fostering support networks and community unity.

The erosion of trust extends beyond local communities to broader societal structures. QAnon's message has left many followers suspicious of fundamental societal pillars, including education, healthcare, and media. Even after followers disengage from QAnon, the lingering distrust may persist, making it difficult for them to fully reintegrate into a society they once viewed as controlled by a malevolent elite. The doubt QAnon has sown in institutional authority doesn't simply vanish; it can color perceptions for years, influencing how people engage with news, public health guidance, and even government initiatives. This ongoing mistrust complicates efforts to rebuild social unity, as followers who leave QAnon may remain hesitant to trust the very institutions that provide essential public services.

The long-term social consequences of QAnon also challenge efforts to address other pressing societal issues. A community polarized by conspiracy theories may struggle to come together on critical topics like climate change, healthcare access, or economic inequality, as differing worldviews prevent meaningful discussion or compromise. QAnon's presence fosters an "us versus them" mentality that pits individuals and groups against each other, undermining the sense of shared responsibility and common purpose that is essential for collective action. In this fractured environment, communities become less resilient, with members viewing those with different beliefs not as fellow citizens but as adversaries.

Rebuilding trust and cohesion after QAnon's influence is a daunting task, requiring time, patience, and dedicated efforts by community leaders, educators, and mental health professionals. For those communities most affected, healing will involve creating spaces for open dialogue, promoting media literacy, and providing support for those who have experienced the fallout of QAnon firsthand. Programs that encourage critical thinking and teach individuals to evaluate information sources can help prevent future conspiracy theories from gaining similar traction. Community-building initiatives that emphasize empathy, mutual respect, and understanding will be essential in restoring the bonds that QAnon has weakened.

In the end, the long-term impact of QAnon is a reminder of the fragility of social trust. A healthy society relies on its members' ability to trust one another, to respect differences, and to work together despite varying beliefs. QAnon has tested these foundations, leaving in its wake a trail of fractured relationships, divided communities, and persistent skepticism. The process of healing will be slow and complex, but it is a necessary journey for communities hoping to move beyond the divisions QAnon has created. Only through sustained efforts to rebuild trust and foster understanding can society begin to repair the damage, creating a stronger, more resilient community capable of withstanding future challenges.

Chapter 10: Dissecting the Evidence: What's True,

1. The Origins of QAnon's Key Theories

The core theories that drive QAnon did not emerge in isolation; they evolved from a complex web of longstanding conspiracy narratives, political ideologies, and cultural anxieties. By tracing the origins of QAnon's primary claims, we can see how each element of the movement draws on past conspiracy theories, giving QAnon an aura of familiarity that makes its claims feel credible to followers. From the concept of a shadowy "deep state" to accusations of elite-run child trafficking rings, QAnon's ideas tap into fears that have existed for decades, if not centuries, reimagined to fit a modern narrative.

The concept of a "deep state"—the idea that a clandestine group of unelected elites secretly controls the government and manipulates events to serve their interests—has roots that go back at least to the Cold War era. During this time, suspicions of hidden influence within the government were common, fueled by real events like McCarthyism, the Watergate scandal, and covert CIA operations. For QAnon, the "deep state" represents a hidden network of corrupt bureaucrats, intelligence officials, and politicians who supposedly manipulate policies and public perception to benefit a small elite. This modern interpretation of the deep state gained traction during the presidency of Donald Trump, who positioned himself as an outsider battling entrenched interests. For QAnon followers, Trump's rhetoric about "draining the swamp" became a rallying cry, and his adversaries were reimagined as shadowy operatives working against the people.

Another central element of QAnon's belief system is the narrative of elite child trafficking rings, which alleges that high-profile figures, particularly in politics, entertainment, and business, are secretly involved in abusing children and participating in global trafficking networks. This claim, while baseless, taps into deep-seated fears about child exploitation. Historical conspiracy theories like the "Satanic Panic" of the 1980s—when rumors of satanic ritual abuse swept the United States—planted the seeds for QAnon's trafficking narrative. During that period, widespread, unfounded allegations claimed that daycare centers, churches, and prominent individuals were involved in satanic abuse rituals, causing a wave of fear and multiple high-profile legal cases. Although largely debunked, these stories left a lasting impact on the public psyche, and QAnon revived these fears, framing them in a way that gave them new life in the digital age.

The role of Hollywood and global elites in QAnon's narrative builds on historical anti-establishment ideas and anti-Semitic tropes, which have long been weaponized to explain societal unrest or inequality. QAnon's claim that a secret group of elites controls world events echoes conspiracy theories like those promoted in *The Protocols of the Elders of Zion*, a fabricated document used for over a century to fuel anti-Semitic beliefs. Although QAnon does not explicitly embrace such language, the underlying structure of the movement's theories aligns with these older conspiracy frameworks, depicting a faceless, powerful enemy that operates above and beyond the reach of ordinary citizens. By framing its narratives in ways that echo these long-standing beliefs, QAnon taps into cultural fears that feel both familiar and menacing.

Real-world events have also played a role in shaping QAnon's theories. High-profile cases like Jeffrey Epstein's arrest for sex trafficking and his suspicious death in custody added fuel to QAnon's claims of elite corruption. Epstein's connections to powerful figures across business, politics, and entertainment created an ideal backdrop for QAnon's trafficking allegations, allowing followers to view his case as proof of a vast network of hidden abuses. In QAnon's narrative, Epstein's death became evidence of a cover-up orchestrated by elites desperate to protect themselves from exposure. This connection to real-world scandals gives QAnon's theories a veneer of plausibility, as followers use actual events as a basis for their beliefs, even if they reinterpret or exaggerate the facts to fit their worldview.

In this way, QAnon's key theories are an amalgamation of historical conspiracy beliefs, contemporary events, and political rhetoric. By weaving together these disparate elements, QAnon offers followers a narrative that feels timeless and universal, drawing on fears and suspicions that have been ingrained in the public consciousness for decades. This synthesis of familiar anxieties with modern events gives QAnon an air of legitimacy that can be compelling to those who feel disillusioned with mainstream explanations. By understanding the origins of QAnon's core theories, we can see how the movement has leveraged both history and current events to construct a worldview that resonates deeply with its followers, tapping into emotions and beliefs that are difficult to shake.

2. Separating Fact from Fiction: Verifiable Elements vs. Pure Speculation

One of the challenges in understanding QAnon's claims is separating the fragments of truth that may be embedded in its narratives from the speculation and outright falsehoods that define much of the movement. QAnon's power lies, in part, in its ability to take kernels of reality—such as high-profile scandals, government secrecy, or elite influence—and weave them into a tapestry of conspiracy that appears plausible to those already inclined to distrust mainstream institutions. By examining QAnon's major claims and identifying what's verifiable versus what's speculative or false, we can better understand why so many find the movement compelling, even when much of its foundation crumbles under scrutiny.

One aspect of QAnon that initially drew followers was its focus on real-world scandals that resonated with the public's existing concerns about corruption and abuse of power. For instance, QAnon's repeated focus on child trafficking aligns with documented instances of trafficking and abuse, such as the highly publicized Jeffrey Epstein case. Epstein's connections to prominent figures across business, entertainment, and politics have fueled longstanding suspicions of elite misconduct, providing fertile ground for QAnon's child trafficking narrative. However, QAnon's followers quickly expand upon these isolated cases, making sweeping claims about widespread, organized abuse rings involving nearly every high-profile figure. While isolated cases of trafficking and abuse are unfortunately real, QAnon's assertions of global, coordinated efforts led by elite networks lack credible evidence, moving the claim from grounded concerns to unfounded conspiracy.

Similarly, QAnon often draws on government secrecy as "evidence" of hidden agendas. Historically, there are real instances of government agencies operating in secrecy—covert military actions, intelligence operations, and classified programs, such as the CIA's MK-Ultra project in the 1950s and '60s, are well-documented examples. QAnon followers frequently cite these past instances of secrecy as justification for believing in a contemporary "deep state" controlling events from behind the scenes. While it's true that governments sometimes operate with limited transparency, QAnon's interpretation escalates this idea into a vast, omnipotent cabal that controls global politics, a claim for which there is no substantive evidence. The fact that the government operates in secrecy in certain areas does not equate to QAnon's assertion of a global conspiracy involving nearly every influential figure in politics, entertainment, and beyond.

QAnon's reliance on misinterpretation also plays a significant role in fueling its narrative. For example, followers often latch onto symbols, phrases, or behaviors they interpret as "signs" of complicity in hidden crimes. A common claim is that hand gestures, logos, or certain word choices are coded messages revealing loyalty to QAnon's alleged cabal of elites. However, these interpretations are largely speculative, with no basis in fact. Symbols and gestures can have multiple meanings depending on context, and QAnon's interpretations often rely on tenuous connections or out-of-context visuals. For instance, followers might interpret a common hand gesture as a sign of allegiance to the alleged cabal, despite it being widely used in other contexts. This practice of assigning hidden meanings to ambiguous signs fosters a "connect-the-dots" mentality that creates the illusion of a coherent conspiracy, even though the connections lack empirical grounding.

QAnon's failure to produce verifiable evidence is further underscored by the inaccuracy of many of its predictions. Since its inception, QAnon has made numerous prophecies, such as dates for mass arrests of high-profile figures or the exposure of "the cabal," none of which have materialized. Despite these repeated failures, QAnon followers often reinterpret these missed predictions, attributing them to purposeful misdirection or "necessary disinformation" to protect Q's plans. While the movement claims to offer privileged access to future events, the repeated inaccuracy of these predictions calls into question the validity of QAnon's sources and methods. Followers' willingness to reinterpret or ignore failed predictions highlights the power of confirmation bias within the movement, as they selectively interpret information to reinforce their beliefs.

Ultimately, QAnon's success in attracting followers stems from its ability to take verifiable concerns—such as instances of government secrecy or cases of elite misconduct—and exaggerate or misinterpret them to create a grand narrative that appeals to those skeptical of mainstream narratives. The movement blurs the line between fact and fiction, drawing followers in with fragments of reality before leading them down a path of increasingly speculative and unsupported claims. For those outside the movement, recognizing the difference between legitimate concerns and conspiratorial distortion is essential in understanding why QAnon has been able to maintain its hold on so many despite a foundation riddled with misinformation. In this way, QAnon's allure becomes clear: it offers a simple explanation for complex issues, weaving together elements of truth with enough fiction to create a narrative that feels both urgent and revelatory to those seeking answers in an uncertain world.

3. The "Research" Methods of QAnon Followers

One of the defining aspects of QAnon is its rallying call for followers to "do their own research." This phrase, which emphasizes personal investigation over reliance on mainstream sources, has a powerful appeal to those who feel disillusioned with traditional media and authority figures. Followers take pride in what they see as independent, critical thinking, sifting through vast amounts of information to uncover "hidden truths" they believe others are too blind or biased to see. However, the research methods employed within QAnon are often flawed and riddled with biases that serve to reinforce rather than challenge the movement's claims. These methods foster a false sense of authority among followers, creating an echo chamber that validates their beliefs while insulating them from counter-evidence.

QAnon's research approach typically begins with followers examining content from internet sources that align with the movement's worldview. Conspiracy-focused websites, YouTube channels, obscure news sites, and social media accounts become primary sources of information. Rather than consulting a range of perspectives or credible sources, followers tend to seek out materials that confirm preexisting suspicions about elite corruption, hidden agendas, or government deception. This selective information gathering, known as confirmation bias, creates a self-reinforcing loop. By choosing sources that align with their beliefs and avoiding those that challenge them, followers build a version of reality that supports QAnon's theories, irrespective of contradictory evidence.

Much of QAnon's "research" relies heavily on cherry-picking data—selecting specific details from real-world events and ignoring those that don't support the desired narrative. A news story about a prominent arrest might be taken out of context and linked to QAnon's central claims about a global cabal, regardless of whether the facts actually support that connection. Minor details, such as specific words or images used in news broadcasts, are often scrutinized for hidden meanings. This hyper-focus on isolated elements allows followers to weave disparate events into a coherent-seeming narrative that matches QAnon's themes. Cherry-picking isn't just a flaw in methodology; it actively distorts the truth, presenting a manipulated version of events that feels compelling because it confirms followers' expectations.

Another common issue in QAnon's research practices is the misuse of logical fallacies, such as correlation implying causation. Followers often mistake coincidence for evidence of conspiracy, interpreting unrelated events as interconnected parts of a grand plan. For example, if two seemingly prominent figures are photographed together, followers may leap to conclusions about their involvement in a hidden scheme, even if there's no substantial connection between them. This pattern of thinking is not unique to QAnon but is characteristic of many conspiracy theories, where coincidences are reinterpreted as meaningful connections. QAnon's community encourages followers to find these "clues" and "connections" in everyday events, reinforcing a sense of uncovering hidden knowledge, even when the evidence is purely circumstantial.

The community aspect of QAnon plays a crucial role in sustaining and validating followers' research efforts. Many QAnon followers join online forums and social media groups where they share findings and theories, creating a support system that rewards their "investigative" efforts. In these spaces, followers' ideas are rarely questioned and are instead met with encouragement, praise, and further elaboration. This environment reinforces followers' beliefs, making them feel as though they are part of a collaborative movement revealing secrets the world isn't ready to face. In reality, these online communities function as echo chambers, where any evidence or perspective that contradicts QAnon's beliefs is dismissed as part of the "mainstream narrative" or as "disinformation" designed to mislead. By engaging in this closed loop of validation, followers become increasingly insulated from outside perspectives, solidifying their commitment to QAnon's worldview.

QAnon's call to "do your own research" appeals to followers' desire for autonomy and intellectual independence, but in practice, it leads to a distorted version of critical thinking. Instead of questioning their own assumptions, followers engage in selective research practices that confirm their beliefs, while the movement's encouragement of confirmation bias and echo chambers stifles true skepticism. In the end, the research methods used within QAnon do not bring followers closer to understanding reality; they create an alternate reality—one that feels empowering but is built on selective interpretation and a rejection of the evidence-based methodologies that are essential to true inquiry. Through these methods, QAnon constructs a world that feels intensely real to its followers, even as it distances them further from the truth.

4. The Role of Debunking and Fact-Checking Efforts

As QAnon's influence grew, efforts to debunk its claims became increasingly essential. Fact-checking organizations, media outlets, independent researchers, and even former QAnon followers have all attempted to counter the spread of QAnon's misinformation by presenting evidence and correcting falsehoods. However, the effectiveness of these efforts has been mixed. While some followers have responded to fact-checking and debunking with skepticism and resistance, others have been able to reevaluate their beliefs when presented with credible, well-reasoned counterpoints. Debunking QAnon requires a nuanced approach, as the movement's foundation is built on a deep distrust of traditional sources, making simple fact-checks often insufficient.

Early debunking efforts focused on providing straightforward corrections to specific QAnon claims, such as dismantling allegations of widespread child trafficking rings involving elites or disproving conspiracy theories surrounding prominent figures. Fact-checkers aimed to present the truth behind each claim, offering concrete evidence to demonstrate that these accusations were false or grossly misinterpreted. Despite the factual basis of these corrections, however, many QAnon followers dismissed them, viewing mainstream media and fact-checking organizations as part of the very "deep state" QAnon warned against. For them, debunking efforts served as confirmation of the movement's narrative: if institutions were working so hard to disprove QAnon, it must mean the movement was onto something important.

In response to this resistance, some researchers and former QAnon followers began adopting alternative strategies to reach those entrenched in the movement. Rather than directly confronting followers with evidence that contradicted their beliefs, these approaches focused on encouraging critical thinking and gently introducing alternative perspectives. Former QAnon adherents who left the movement have been particularly effective in these efforts, using their own experiences to build rapport with current followers and explain why they ultimately abandoned QAnon. By sharing stories of their own disillusionment, these former members help active followers see that it is possible to leave without losing the sense of purpose that brought them to QAnon in the first place.

Social media platforms have also played a key role in attempting to curb the spread of QAnon through moderation and labeling practices. Major platforms like Facebook, Twitter, and YouTube have implemented measures to label, downrank, or remove QAnon-related content, especially posts that contain overt misinformation or that could incite harm. Facebook and Instagram, for example, introduced labels that notify users when a post has been debunked, while YouTube removed entire QAnon channels that spread misinformation about COVID-19, elections, and child trafficking. Twitter has suspended QAnon-related accounts and banned QAnon-related hashtags in an effort to reduce the movement's visibility. While these measures have limited the reach of QAnon content on mainstream platforms, they have also pushed some followers to fringe sites, where content is often even more extreme and un-moderated.

The challenge of effectively debunking QAnon lies in the movement's deep-seated distrust of traditional authority figures and mainstream narratives. QAnon followers often reject corrections not based on the quality of evidence but on their perception of the source. As a result, fact-checking efforts must navigate the complex dynamics of belief and trust, understanding that the simple presentation of facts may not be enough. Researchers and mental health professionals who work with families affected by QAnon emphasize the importance of empathy and patience, encouraging loved ones to approach debunking not as an adversarial confrontation but as a gradual process that involves listening, asking open-ended questions, and respecting the follower's autonomy.

One of the most effective debunking strategies has been to focus on the failed predictions within QAnon's own narrative. Since its inception, QAnon has promoted numerous dates for supposed mass arrests, revelations, or political upheavals—none of which have come to pass. By highlighting these discrepancies, some former followers have been able to recognize inconsistencies within the movement, leading them to question the validity of other claims. For those willing to entertain these doubts, acknowledging the failed predictions can be the first step in loosening QAnon's hold. However, this approach requires delicacy, as pressing a follower too forcefully on these inconsistencies can trigger defensive reactions that reinforce their beliefs.

The debunking and fact-checking efforts surrounding QAnon reveal a fundamental lesson about countering conspiracy theories: facts alone are rarely enough to dismantle deeply held beliefs. Successful interventions often require empathy, personal connection, and a willingness to engage in open dialogue. By meeting followers where they are and respecting the complexity of their beliefs, debunking efforts can create openings for critical reflection, planting seeds that may one day help followers re-evaluate their involvement in QAnon. In this way, the fight against misinformation becomes as much about understanding human psychology as it is about establishing the truth, offering a path forward in an era where trust is as valuable as truth itself.

5. The Psychological Appeal of QAnon's Claims Despite Lack of Evidence

Despite a lack of credible evidence to support its central claims, QAnon has captivated millions by tapping into fundamental psychological needs and biases. For many, the movement provides a sense of purpose, belonging, and control over a chaotic world, which makes it uniquely resistant to fact-checking and debunking efforts. The power of QAnon lies less in the factual basis of its claims and more in the emotional and psychological resonance it holds for followers. Through its engaging narratives, QAnon addresses deep-seated desires for meaning and certainty, even as it pulls followers further from objective reality.

At the heart of QAnon's appeal is its promise of a simplified explanation for complex societal problems. In a world filled with uncertainty, QAnon offers a clear-cut narrative: good versus evil, heroes versus villains. For followers, this simplicity is comforting. It provides an accessible framework for understanding why things go wrong, attributing all suffering and corruption to a single cabal of elites working in secrecy. This narrative relieves followers of the burden of grappling with ambiguity, allowing them to believe that society's troubles can be traced back to identifiable culprits. In doing so, QAnon gives its followers the satisfaction of feeling like they have "uncovered" the truth, freeing them from the discomfort of uncertainty and complexity.

QAnon also fulfills a powerful desire for community and belonging, particularly in an era where social fragmentation and isolation are common. For many followers, QAnon communities provide a support network, a place where they feel seen and understood. Within these groups, they find people who share their worldview, creating bonds that feel meaningful and validating. This sense of camaraderie is especially appealing to those who may feel disconnected from traditional social structures or disillusioned with mainstream society. The shared mission of "awakening" others reinforces these connections, creating an "in-group" mentality that strengthens loyalty to QAnon and intensifies the feeling of being part of a special, enlightened community.

The psychological mechanisms of confirmation bias and group-think also play critical roles in maintaining followers' attachment to QAnon. Once individuals begin to engage with QAnon content, they tend to seek out information that aligns with their beliefs and dismiss information that challenges it. This process, known as confirmation bias, fuels followers' conviction, making them more likely to reject counter-evidence or fact-checks as "part of the cover-up." Additionally, groupthink within QAnon communities reinforces these beliefs, as followers surround themselves with people who echo and validate their ideas. In this environment, questioning or dissenting voices are rare, and those who challenge the movement's claims risk being ostracized. This dynamic keeps followers entrenched in QAnon's worldview, as the need for social acceptance and validation outweighs the incentive to critically evaluate the movement's claims.

QAnon also appeals to individuals' desire to feel special or "chosen." By presenting followers as warriors in an information war, QAnon gives them a sense of purpose and heroism. Followers see themselves as part of a global mission to uncover hidden truths and protect society from a sinister elite. This role provides a deep sense of meaning, allowing them to view their research and online activism as acts of courage and defiance. In this way, QAnon provides not only an explanation for why the world feels chaotic but also an empowering role for its followers within that chaos. This identity as "truth-seekers" or "digital soldiers" becomes central to followers' self-perception, making it difficult for them to disengage from the movement without feeling they are abandoning a significant part of their identity.

Perhaps most powerfully, QAnon satisfies a basic psychological need for control in a world that often feels unpredictable and overwhelming. By framing events as part of a hidden plan, QAnon gives followers a sense that they understand the "real" reasons behind societal upheaval, which can be more comforting than confronting the randomness and complexity of life. QAnon followers feel they are one step ahead, able to see the patterns and connections that others miss, which provides a feeling of agency that can be deeply reassuring. This sense of control becomes a buffer against the anxiety and helplessness that so many feel in the face of political and social instability, allowing followers to believe that they have the power to make a difference, even if only by sharing their beliefs online.

In the end, QAnon's appeal is not rooted in factual accuracy but in its ability to meet the emotional and psychological needs of its followers. By offering clear explanations, a sense of belonging, and a feeling of empowerment, QAnon provides followers with an identity and a purpose, making it resistant to traditional forms of debunking. The movement's strength lies in the fact that it resonates on a personal, often subconscious level, appealing to universal human desires for certainty, connection, and control. For many followers, giving up these beliefs would mean losing a sense of purpose and community, which is why QAnon persists, even as its claims are repeatedly disproven. Understanding these psychological dynamics is crucial for anyone seeking to address QAnon's influence, as it reveals that the movement's appeal lies not in its truthfulness but in its power to fulfill human needs that facts alone cannot satisfy.

Chapter 11: The Fight Against Disinformation

1. Government Initiatives to Combat Disinformation

In recent years, governments worldwide have recognized the growing threat that disinformation poses to public trust, national security, and social cohesion. As false information spreads rapidly online, often fueled by divisive narratives, governments have mobilized to address the issue through a range of initiatives. These efforts include creating specialized task forces, introducing legislation, promoting public awareness campaigns, and collaborating with other nations to tackle cross-border disinformation. The challenge, however, lies in balancing these measures with the preservation of free speech, ensuring that the fight against misinformation does not inadvertently infringe upon civil liberties.

Many governments have established dedicated task forces or units specifically designed to monitor and counteract disinformation. In the United States, for example, agencies like the Cybersecurity and Infrastructure Security Agency (CISA) play a central role in identifying and responding to threats of misinformation, particularly around elections and critical infrastructure. CISA has launched campaigns, such as "Rumor Control," to debunk election-related falsehoods, providing citizens with factual information to counter misleading narratives. These government initiatives aim to maintain public confidence in the democratic process by proactively addressing common sources of confusion or falsehood.

Across the Atlantic, European governments have implemented their own anti-disinformation strategies. The European Union's "Action Plan Against Disinformation," launched in 2018, is a comprehensive effort to counter false information across EU member states. The plan includes establishing rapid alert systems for potential disinformation campaigns, coordinating responses among member states, and working closely with tech companies to limit the spread of false narratives. Additionally, the European Union's East StratCom Task Force, with its "EUvsDisinfo" project, specifically targets disinformation campaigns originating from outside the EU, particularly from sources linked to Russia. By identifying and addressing these foreign influence campaigns, the EU aims to protect its member states from the destabilizing effects of false information aimed at dividing European societies.

International cooperation has proven essential in combating cross-border disinformation, as misinformation often transcends national boundaries and can have global implications. Initiatives like the Global Partnership on Artificial Intelligence (GPAI) bring together countries to develop ethical guidelines and technical standards for AI-driven disinformation tools, such as deepfakes and automated bots. Similarly, organizations like NATO have established frameworks for member countries to share information about disinformation threats, particularly those targeting national security or critical infrastructure. This international collaboration is vital, as coordinated efforts allow countries to address disinformation that may be aimed at influencing multiple nations simultaneously, such as election interference or pandemic-related misinformation.

Despite these efforts, governments face significant challenges in curbing disinformation without infringing upon free speech. Democratic societies are built on the principle of open discourse, where diverse opinions can be freely shared, even if they are controversial or unpopular. However, disinformation campaigns often blur the line between free speech and harmful falsehoods that undermine societal stability. Governments must tread carefully, ensuring that their actions do not lead to censorship or suppression of legitimate dissent. For instance, laws aimed at preventing the spread of disinformation may unintentionally stifle independent journalism or alternative viewpoints, particularly in cases where information is later found to be true or debatable.

In addressing these complexities, some governments have introduced transparency and accountability measures, rather than outright censorship. For example, instead of banning certain content, authorities might require platforms to label or downrank misleading posts, allowing users to access information while providing context about its accuracy. Public awareness campaigns have also emerged as an alternative approach, educating citizens on how to identify and report disinformation without limiting their access to information. The UK, for example, has launched initiatives like "Don't Feed the Beast," which encourages people to pause and evaluate content before sharing it, promoting a culture of critical thinking and self-regulation.

Ultimately, government initiatives to combat disinformation represent a delicate balancing act. Efforts to limit the spread of false information must be weighed against the need to protect freedom of expression and prevent government overreach. While there is no one-size-fits-all solution, a combination of proactive monitoring, international collaboration, transparency measures, and public education appears to be the most effective strategy in addressing the complex and evolving challenge of disinformation in today's digital landscape. As the threat of disinformation continues to grow, governments worldwide will need to remain adaptable, refining their approaches to safeguard both public trust and democratic values.

2. The Role of Tech Companies in Regulating Content

As disinformation has proliferated across social media and digital platforms, tech companies have found themselves at the forefront of the battle to curb its spread. Platforms like Facebook, Twitter, and YouTube, which collectively host billions of users, serve as the primary channels through which disinformation circulates, making these companies essential players in the fight against false narratives. To address the issue, tech companies have implemented a variety of strategies, including content moderation, algorithm adjustments, labeling of false information, and partnerships with fact-checking organizations. However, these measures come with their own set of challenges, as tech companies must balance the need to protect their users from harmful misinformation with the imperative to uphold free speech and maintain user trust.

Content moderation remains one of the most direct methods tech companies use to control disinformation. Facebook, for example, employs teams of human moderators alongside artificial intelligence (AI) systems to review posts that may contain false or harmful information. This approach is complemented by partnerships with independent fact-checkers, who help assess the accuracy of content flagged by the platform's algorithms. When a post is deemed false, it may be labeled, downranked to limit its visibility, or, in extreme cases, removed entirely. YouTube similarly relies on a combination of AI and human moderation, with policies in place to take down videos that promote dangerous conspiracies or spread harmful falsehoods about issues like public health. By moderating content in this way, tech companies aim to prevent disinformation from reaching large audiences before it can take hold.

Algorithm adjustments have also become a crucial part of tech companies' strategies to combat disinformation. Many platforms use algorithms that prioritize content based on user engagement, meaning that posts with high levels of interaction are more likely to appear in users' feeds. However, disinformation often generates significant engagement, as sensational or emotionally charged content tends to attract likes, shares, and comments. In response, companies like Twitter have made adjustments to their algorithms to prevent misinformation from being amplified. Twitter's algorithm now deprioritizes tweets flagged as misleading, reducing their reach and impact without outright censoring the content. Similarly, Facebook has modified its News Feed algorithm to prioritize content from reliable sources over sensational or misleading posts, aiming to strike a balance between engagement and information integrity.

Labeling misinformation is another common approach, as it allows tech companies to provide context without directly removing content. For instance, Twitter and Facebook frequently use labels to indicate when posts contain disputed or potentially false information, particularly on sensitive topics like COVID-19, election integrity, and major political events. These labels often link to verified sources or fact-checks that clarify the information, giving users the option to verify the content themselves. This approach preserves the availability of diverse viewpoints while encouraging users to consider the credibility of the information before sharing it. YouTube, too, has adopted this approach, adding "context panels" that appear below videos on controversial topics, offering additional sources and background information. By labeling misinformation rather than censoring it, tech companies aim to inform users without restricting access to information.

Despite these efforts, tech companies face considerable backlash and accusations of censorship. Many users, particularly those who support conspiracy theories or alternative narratives, see content moderation and labeling as attempts to control or suppress free speech. For instance, Twitter's decision to ban certain high-profile accounts for repeated misinformation violations sparked a public debate over the role of tech companies in regulating speech. Critics argue that platforms are exercising too much power over public discourse, while advocates believe tech companies have a responsibility to prevent harm caused by disinformation. This tension underscores the challenge tech companies face in maintaining user trust; by intervening in what appears in users' feeds, platforms risk alienating those who believe their perspectives are being unfairly targeted.

Moreover, the technical and logistical challenges of moderating disinformation at scale are significant. Platforms like Facebook and YouTube host billions of posts daily, making it difficult to identify and address every instance of misinformation in real time. While AI systems can help flag suspicious content, they are far from perfect and sometimes fail to differentiate between satire, opinion, and outright falsehoods. Additionally, disinformation spreaders often adapt to moderation practices, using coded language or shifting to fringe platforms to evade detection. As a result, tech companies must continuously update their strategies to stay ahead of these evolving tactics, a process that requires constant innovation and vigilance.

In the end, tech companies occupy a challenging position in the fight against disinformation. They wield significant influence over public discourse, and their efforts to curb false information are essential in preventing the spread of harmful narratives. However, the line between moderation and censorship remains a contentious issue, one that requires tech companies to make difficult decisions about which content to limit or promote. As they continue to refine their approaches, tech companies must balance their commitment to accuracy with the principles of open dialogue and free speech, knowing that their actions have far-reaching implications for both individual users and society as a whole. In this ongoing effort, tech companies are not only combating disinformation but also navigating the complex role they play as gatekeepers of information in the digital age.

3. Media Literacy and Education: Building Resilience Against Misinformation

One of the most effective strategies in the fight against disinformation is equipping individuals with the tools to recognize and evaluate information critically. Media literacy programs, which teach people how to assess the credibility of information sources, identify biases, and detect misleading content, are increasingly seen as essential in today's information-rich society. These educational efforts aim to build a population resilient to the effects of misinformation, empowering people to navigate complex media landscapes with discernment. By promoting critical thinking and fostering a healthy skepticism, media literacy and education initiatives provide a long-term solution to the challenge of disinformation.

Media literacy begins in schools, where students are taught to analyze information from a young age. In response to the rise of disinformation, many educational systems have adapted their curriculums to include lessons on digital literacy, focusing on helping students discern credible sources and recognize tactics used in spreading misinformation. For instance, students learn how to distinguish between fact-based news and opinion pieces, understand the basics of reliable sourcing, and assess the intent behind headlines or social media posts. Through exercises like evaluating mock news articles or identifying logical fallacies, students develop the skills needed to approach information with a critical eye. These lessons foster awareness that extends beyond school, preparing students to engage with digital content as responsible consumers throughout their lives.

Universities and non-profit organizations have also played a significant role in promoting media literacy. Programs like Stanford University's Civic Online Reasoning and the News Literacy Project offer resources, workshops, and curricula that teach individuals how to assess information online. These initiatives provide people with tools to identify manipulated images, verify sources, and fact-check claims, all while encouraging a balanced perspective that avoids overcorrection into distrust of all media. For example, the News Literacy Project's Checkology platform provides interactive modules that guide users through common misinformation techniques, helping them to build skills they can apply in real-world situations. By making these resources widely accessible, universities and organizations hope to cultivate a more informed and resilient public capable of discerning fact from fiction.

Effective media literacy programs acknowledge the importance of fostering a healthy skepticism without descending into cynicism. Teaching individuals to question information responsibly involves helping them understand the difference between critical analysis and blanket distrust. This balanced approach encourages people to ask questions about the information they consume while also recognizing the value of credible journalism and reliable sources. By teaching people to look for evidence, corroborate facts across multiple sources, and recognize signs of manipulation, media literacy programs empower individuals to become informed decision-makers without fostering hostility toward legitimate news and information outlets.

Targeting diverse age groups and demographics is also crucial to the success of media literacy efforts. Young people, who are often the most active on social media, benefit from early education in media literacy, as they encounter a significant amount of unfiltered information online. However, older adults are equally vulnerable to disinformation, particularly as they may be less familiar with digital platforms or the specific techniques used to spread false information. Recognizing this, some media literacy initiatives have been developed specifically for older audiences, such as workshops provided by libraries or community centers. These programs address unique challenges faced by older adults, offering practical guidance on navigating digital news sources and social media while helping them become more comfortable with verifying information online.

As media literacy gains traction, governments and communities are also advocating for media literacy to be integrated into formal education policy, seeing it as a necessary skill for informed citizenship. Countries like Finland and Sweden have made media literacy an official part of their national education systems, a move that has led to higher resilience against misinformation among their populations. In Finland, for example, media literacy education begins in primary school and is reinforced throughout students' education, resulting in a citizenry that is better equipped to handle misinformation. Other countries are observing these successes and exploring similar approaches, recognizing that an informed and critical-thinking population is essential for a healthy democracy.

Media literacy and education are essential components in the long-term fight against misinformation. While fact-checking and content moderation address disinformation reactively, media literacy provides a proactive solution, building a foundation of knowledge and skepticism that helps people independently evaluate the credibility of what they see and read. By promoting media literacy at all levels—from classrooms to community programs—society can cultivate a culture of informed, critical consumers who are less susceptible to manipulation. In an age where information is abundant but trust is scarce, media literacy stands as a crucial tool in empowering individuals to discern truth from falsehood and engage thoughtfully with the world around them.

4. Community and Grassroots Efforts to Address Disinformation

While governments and tech companies play prominent roles in the fight against disinformation, grassroots and community-based initiatives have proven equally critical. These localized efforts leverage trust within communities to educate individuals, dispel myths, and combat the spread of harmful misinformation. By using peer-to-peer communication, community leaders, and culturally tailored approaches, grassroots initiatives can address disinformation in ways that larger, top-down efforts sometimes struggle to achieve. Community-based programs tap into the power of personal relationships and local networks to foster understanding, encourage critical thinking, and rebuild trust in credible information sources.

One of the most powerful aspects of grassroots efforts is their ability to reach people within their own social circles, where trust is often stronger than in national or institutional sources. For example, individuals may be more willing to reconsider a false claim when they hear a counter-argument from a friend, family member, or respected local figure rather than a faceless institution. This dynamic can be especially effective in close-knit communities where personal relationships carry significant weight. Community-based programs capitalize on these dynamics by training volunteers to facilitate open discussions, encourage skepticism toward unverified information, and promote fact-checking. This person-to-person approach creates an environment where individuals feel more comfortable discussing their beliefs and are more open to considering alternative perspectives.

Local organizations and community leaders also play a pivotal role in addressing disinformation, particularly within minority or marginalized groups who may distrust mainstream media or government sources. Community leaders, such as religious figures, local activists, or influential business owners, have built rapport with their communities over years or even decades, making their voices highly respected. By partnering with these trusted figures, grassroots initiatives can convey accurate information in ways that feel authentic and accessible to the community. For instance, during the COVID-19 pandemic, some communities turned to local religious leaders to counter vaccine misinformation. These leaders held informational sessions, dispelled myths, and addressed questions in culturally sensitive ways, helping individuals make informed health decisions. This approach not only built trust but also empowered communities to seek reliable information independently.

Some of the most effective grassroots initiatives use creative, culturally specific methods to engage with their audiences. In multilingual or multicultural communities, translating fact-checking materials into local languages and tailoring messaging to cultural contexts can make all the difference. For example, workshops in immigrant communities might address topics in multiple languages and use culturally relevant examples to discuss the dangers of misinformation. Some organizations even employ local art, storytelling, or theatre to illustrate the impact of disinformation, creating an engaging and relatable experience for participants. By meeting people where they are—linguistically, culturally, and socially—these efforts break down barriers to understanding and foster resilience against misleading narratives.

Grassroots campaigns have also embraced digital platforms to counter disinformation effectively. In some cases, volunteers organize social media groups, WhatsApp chains, or Telegram channels where they share verified information, debunk local rumors, and promote healthy skepticism. These groups create online spaces where people can discuss their concerns, ask questions, and receive accurate responses in real-time. For instance, during elections, local initiatives might use these digital channels to fact-check viral political claims, helping community members make informed voting decisions. This peer-driven model proves particularly effective in regions where disinformation thrives on private messaging platforms, as it empowers community members to become fact-checkers within their own networks.

A unique strength of grassroots efforts is their adaptability. Unlike large-scale initiatives, which can be slow to pivot, grassroots campaigns are often more flexible, allowing them to respond quickly to emerging misinformation. If a rumor spreads within a community, these local networks can act swiftly, sending out clarifications and corrections before the disinformation takes hold. For example, during natural disasters or public health crises, grassroots networks have provided timely updates and corrected misinformation that might otherwise cause panic or hinder effective responses. This real-time agility allows communities to remain informed and better equipped to handle misinformation as it arises.

In an era of widespread disinformation, community and grassroots initiatives bring a human element to the fight against misinformation, bridging the gap between large-scale institutional efforts and individuals who may feel disconnected from mainstream sources. By leveraging trust within communities, promoting peer-to-peer education, and tailoring efforts to cultural contexts, these grassroots campaigns empower people to think critically and make informed choices. These initiatives demonstrate that the fight against disinformation is not just a top-down battle; it is also a collective effort that thrives on the strength of personal relationships, cultural awareness, and the commitment of everyday individuals to protect truth and foster understanding in their own communities.

5. Evolving Tactics of Disinformation Spreaders and Countermeasures

As efforts to combat disinformation become more sophisticated, those spreading false information have adapted their tactics to stay one step ahead. From deepfake technology and bot networks to encrypted messaging and anonymous accounts, disinformation spreaders are continually refining their methods to evade detection and increase their reach. This constant evolution presents a significant challenge for governments, tech companies, and grassroots organizations working to counter misinformation. To keep pace, they must innovate and adapt, employing advanced tools and agile strategies to address new threats in real time.

One of the most troubling advances in disinformation tactics is the rise of deepfake technology. Deepfakes, which use artificial intelligence to create hyper-realistic but entirely fabricated videos, have the potential to blur the line between truth and fiction like never before. For instance, a deepfake video depicting a prominent figure saying or doing something they never actually did can quickly go viral, influencing public opinion before it can be debunked. Deepfakes have the power to erode trust in visual media, making it increasingly difficult for viewers to differentiate between real and manipulated content. In response, researchers and tech companies are developing detection tools that analyze visual data for signs of manipulation, such as inconsistencies in lighting or unnatural facial movements. While these tools have made progress, the technology behind deepfakes is advancing rapidly, creating an arms race between disinformation spreaders and those working to debunk their fabrications.

Automated bots and networks of fake accounts have also become essential tools for amplifying disinformation. These bots can generate thousands of posts or retweets within minutes, pushing misleading content into trending topics and making it appear more popular and credible than it actually is. This tactic, known as "astroturfing," creates the illusion of widespread public support or outrage, manipulating public perception and influencing media coverage. To combat bot-driven disinformation, social media platforms have invested in AI algorithms that identify patterns of inauthentic behavior, such as rapid posting or the use of identical language across multiple accounts. By identifying and suspending these accounts, platforms can limit the reach of disinformation campaigns. However, disinformation spreaders continually adjust their bot tactics, using more sophisticated networks and artificial personas that blend in with genuine users, making them harder to detect.

Private messaging apps and encrypted platforms present another layer of complexity in the fight against disinformation. Platforms like WhatsApp, Telegram, and Signal allow users to share information within closed, encrypted groups, making it nearly impossible for moderators to monitor content or intervene in real time. During elections, natural disasters, and public health crises, these private groups have become hotbeds for misinformation, as false claims can spread quickly among close-knit networks. In response, some governments and organizations have launched public awareness campaigns specifically targeting users of these apps, encouraging them to verify information before sharing. Additionally, in regions where misinformation on private platforms poses a significant threat, governments have partnered with tech companies to introduce tools that flag widely forwarded messages, alerting users that the content may not be trustworthy. These efforts aim to limit the spread of misinformation while respecting user privacy and the encrypted nature of these platforms.

Emerging technologies are also being developed to counter these evolving tactics. Real-time fact-checking tools and content verification technologies are among the newest countermeasures in this ongoing battle. For example, some news organizations have begun using blockchain technology to track the origin and distribution of news stories, providing a transparent chain of information that allows users to verify a source's credibility. Additionally, fact-checking software embedded within social media platforms now cross-references content with reputable databases to flag and label potentially misleading posts before they go viral. These technologies represent promising advancements in the fight against disinformation, though their effectiveness depends on widespread adoption and continued refinement to keep up with disinformation spreaders' latest tactics.

Disinformation campaigns have also taken advantage of shifting cultural and political landscapes, often using emotionally charged issues to ignite division. For instance, during elections, disinformation spreaders focus on polarizing topics like immigration, race, and national identity, knowing that emotional content is more likely to be shared. They exploit societal divides by crafting messages that resonate with specific groups, creating targeted narratives that reinforce existing biases and grievances. Recognizing this trend, some organizations have developed counter-narrative campaigns that address divisive topics head-on, providing accurate information in a way that respects the concerns of affected communities. By addressing the underlying emotional drivers of disinformation, these campaigns aim to reduce the appeal of misinformation and promote more constructive, fact-based dialogue.

The constantly evolving tactics of disinformation spreaders make the fight against false information a dynamic and ongoing challenge. As long as new methods emerge, countermeasures must adapt accordingly, combining technological innovation with social awareness and media literacy. The battle against disinformation is not solely about debunking false claims; it is about creating a resilient society capable of critically evaluating information in a fast-paced, interconnected world. Governments, tech companies, community leaders, and individuals all play a role in this effort, as each contributes to a larger ecosystem dedicated to protecting truth and fostering trust. In this rapidly changing landscape, the fight against disinformation is not just about countering today's falsehoods but also about building a foundation of resilience that will withstand the tactics of tomorrow.

Chapter 12: What Comes Next: QAnon's Future

1. **Evolution of the Movement: Adaptation and Persistence**
As QAnon faces increasing opposition from social media platforms, fact-checkers, and government agencies, the movement has shown a remarkable ability to adapt and persist. Despite attempts to debunk its core beliefs and restrict its spread online, QAnon has continued to attract followers by reshaping its narrative to stay relevant in changing political and social climates. This adaptability suggests that, rather than disappearing, QAnon may continue to evolve, morphing into new forms that align with current events and public sentiments.

One of the most effective ways QAnon has adapted is by reframing its beliefs to align with new developments in politics and society. Followers who once focused on specific predictions that failed to materialize, such as mass arrests or public "revelations," have shifted their focus to broader themes like government corruption, public health concerns, and elite manipulation. By doing so, QAnon has managed to retain its appeal even as its initial promises went unfulfilled. For example, during the COVID-19 pandemic, many QAnon followers began to incorporate anti-vaccine and anti-lockdown messages into their beliefs, claiming these measures were part of a broader plot by elites to control the population. This flexibility in adapting to current events has allowed QAnon to remain relevant and attract new followers who are disillusioned with mainstream narratives.

Another aspect of QAnon's evolution is its increasing fragmentation. As platforms crack down on QAnon content and as its central figure, "Q," becomes less active, followers have started to form smaller, more localized groups with slightly different focuses and interpretations. Some groups emphasize spirituality, framing QAnon's mission as part of a cosmic struggle between good and evil. Others adopt a more political stance, rallying against perceived overreach by governments or calling for alternative political movements. This fragmentation enables QAnon to spread within different communities, adapting its message to resonate with specific audiences. While this decentralization might dilute QAnon's core ideology, it also makes the movement harder to combat, as it becomes less reliant on any single source or central narrative.

QAnon's ability to merge with other conspiracy theories further strengthens its resilience. Followers are known to absorb ideas from other movements, including theories about globalist agendas, anti-vaccine activism, and "great reset" conspiracies, which claim that elites are manipulating world events to establish a new world order. By merging with these other narratives, QAnon has broadened its appeal, creating a kind of "big tent" for conspiracy theorists who may not align with its original claims but find common ground in its anti-establishment tone. This flexibility not only attracts followers from other conspiracy movements but also allows QAnon to tap into existing communities with shared anxieties about power and control, making the movement more expansive and interconnected.

QAnon's adaptability also extends to its online presence, where followers continue to find ways to communicate and share content despite increased moderation. As mainstream platforms like Twitter, Facebook, and YouTube implement stricter policies against QAnon, many followers have migrated to fringe platforms such as Gab, Parler, and Telegram, which offer fewer restrictions. These platforms provide a safe haven for followers, allowing QAnon narratives to persist and evolve outside the scrutiny of more regulated environments. Additionally, QAnon supporters have developed new methods to evade detection on mainstream platforms, such as using coded language or alternative hashtags that fly under the radar of automated content filters. This ingenuity in adapting to digital constraints underscores QAnon's resilience in the face of increasing online censorship.

Ultimately, QAnon's evolution speaks to its resilience as a social movement. While many conspiracies fade over time, QAnon has adapted to meet the shifting concerns and fears of its followers, ensuring its continued relevance. As long as societal anxieties and distrust of institutions persist, QAnon is likely to find new ways to reinvent itself and attract followers who are searching for answers outside of traditional narratives. This adaptability is both a strength and a challenge for those attempting to counter the movement, as each new form that QAnon takes may require different strategies to address. In the coming years, it is likely that QAnon will continue to persist—not necessarily as a single, unified movement but as a constantly shifting network of beliefs that evolve to fit the fears and suspicions of the moment.

2. Influence on Future Conspiracy Theories

QAnon's lasting impact may not only be in its own persistence but in how it shapes the landscape of future conspiracy theories. QAnon has introduced a highly effective framework for engaging followers and building loyalty, combining decentralized leadership, digital mobilization, and an evolving narrative. By doing so, it has created a template for future conspiracies, with tactics and structures that can be easily adapted and applied to new topics, beliefs, and movements. This model of conspiracy thinking, pioneered by QAnon, will likely influence other groups, encouraging a new generation of conspiracy theories that adopt similar techniques to attract and maintain devoted followings.

One of QAnon's most notable contributions to the conspiracy landscape is its leaderless, decentralized structure. Unlike previous conspiracies led by specific individuals or groups, QAnon operates without a clear authority figure, which has made it exceptionally difficult to dismantle. Followers receive messages from "Q"—an anonymous figure whose cryptic posts are open to interpretation and require "decoding." This ambiguity allows followers to draw their own conclusions, effectively becoming active participants in shaping the movement's beliefs. As a result, QAnon is self-sustaining; followers themselves become leaders, influencers, and interpreters within their communities. Future conspiracy theories may adopt this model of decentralized leadership, encouraging followers to participate in "research" and interpret open-ended clues, creating a movement that feels both democratic and deeply personal.

QAnon has also demonstrated the power of digital mobilization through social media, messaging apps, and online communities. QAnon followers have leveraged digital platforms to create a vibrant community that shares information, builds relationships, and reinforces beliefs. Future conspiracy theories will likely follow QAnon's lead by using social media algorithms to spread their message quickly, taking advantage of the same digital tools and techniques. QAnon's early followers spread their message across Facebook groups, Twitter hashtags, and YouTube channels, reaching new audiences and encouraging engagement through emotionally charged content. Even as platforms crack down on disinformation, alternative and encrypted messaging services like Telegram and Signal provide spaces where these communities can flourish without interference. This use of digital mobilization will likely become a staple of conspiracy theories to come, as it allows movements to maintain a strong sense of community and collective identity online.

Another significant aspect of QAnon's influence is its capacity to merge with and adapt to other conspiracy theories, effectively becoming an umbrella movement. By absorbing beliefs about globalist agendas, anti-vaccine sentiments, and various "deep state" theories, QAnon has managed to appeal to a wide range of followers, each drawn to a different aspect of the narrative. This fusion of different conspiracies has created a broader, more flexible worldview, one that is capable of evolving in response to changing political or social climates. Future conspiracy theories will likely adopt a similar approach, incorporating and building upon existing ideas to create more inclusive narratives. This allows them to attract a diverse following and sustain interest over time, as new ideas and claims keep the movement's content dynamic and engaging.

QAnon's method of building loyalty by creating an "in-group" of followers who see themselves as enlightened truth-seekers is another legacy that future conspiracy theories may replicate. QAnon has cultivated a community where followers feel part of an exclusive club, one with special knowledge and insight denied to the "mainstream." This insider mentality provides followers with a sense of purpose and belonging, reinforcing their commitment to the movement. Future conspiracies may use similar tactics, framing their narratives as an exclusive truth that only a select few can access and understand. By making followers feel unique and "chosen," these movements can foster loyalty that is resistant to outside criticism and highly resilient to debunking efforts.

In addition to these structural and strategic influences, QAnon has also normalized certain kinds of conspiratorial thinking in public discourse. Ideas like the "deep state," hidden cabals of elites, and coded messages from insiders have become common elements in online conversations and pop culture. QAnon's language and symbols, such as "Where We Go One, We Go All" (WWG1WGA), have filtered into broader social media, creating a sense of familiarity and even legitimacy for these concepts. This normalization makes it easier for future conspiracies to gain traction, as they can use similar language and symbols that are already familiar to the public. By embedding these concepts in everyday discourse, QAnon has lowered the threshold for future conspiracy theories, enabling new movements to rise more quickly by tapping into pre-existing ideas and language.

As conspiracy theories continue to adapt and evolve, QAnon's influence will likely persist, shaping the tactics and structures of future movements. QAnon's innovations in decentralized leadership, digital mobilization, multi-conspiracy integration, in-group loyalty, and normalization of conspiracy thinking have provided a durable template that others are likely to follow. Future conspiracies will draw from these strategies, creating movements that feel participatory, empowering, and deeply engaging for followers. In this way, QAnon's legacy may extend beyond its own followers, seeding a new era of conspiracy theories that are increasingly difficult to counter and dismantle, as they capitalize on the powerful sense of belonging, purpose, and "insider" knowledge that have come to define modern conspiracy culture.

3. The Role of Technology: Amplification or Containment

Technology has been both a powerful amplifier and a critical containment tool for QAnon, and its future will continue to be shaped by technological advances. On the one hand, social media platforms, messaging apps, and algorithms have fueled QAnon's growth, allowing it to reach a global audience almost instantly. On the other, technology also holds the potential to curb QAnon's influence, as advancements in content moderation, fact-checking, and misinformation detection evolve. Whether technology will ultimately serve to amplify or contain QAnon depends on how tech companies, governments, and users respond to new digital tools and emerging threats.

One of the primary ways technology has amplified QAnon is through social media algorithms, which prioritize content that generates high engagement—likes, shares, comments, and retweets. Conspiracy theories like QAnon thrive on sensationalist, emotionally charged content, and social media algorithms amplify this type of content because it keeps users engaged. When followers share posts containing QAnon theories, those posts often reach a wider audience because algorithms boost them based on their engagement metrics. The viral nature of social media has allowed QAnon to expand from niche internet forums to major platforms like Facebook, Twitter, and Instagram, reaching audiences who may not actively seek out conspiracy content but are exposed to it through friends, trending topics, or recommended posts.

Private messaging apps and encrypted platforms have also provided spaces where QAnon followers can connect and share information without outside interference. Apps like Telegram, WhatsApp, and Signal are widely used by QAnon followers to organize, spread information, and avoid content moderation policies imposed by mainstream platforms. These closed networks allow misinformation to spread unchecked, creating echo chambers where followers can share unverified claims with minimal risk of being flagged or fact-checked. Encrypted messaging apps pose a particular challenge because they protect user privacy, making it difficult for platforms or authorities to monitor or counter the spread of misinformation within these spaces. As a result, the migration of QAnon followers to encrypted platforms may strengthen the movement by creating insular communities where conspiracy theories flourish without resistance.

In response to these challenges, tech companies have increased their efforts to contain QAnon's influence through improved content moderation and the development of more sophisticated algorithms to detect and reduce misinformation. Platforms like Twitter and Facebook now use AI-driven tools to identify QAnon-related content, label it as misinformation, and, in some cases, remove it entirely. YouTube has taken a similar approach, removing entire channels that spread QAnon content. By refining their moderation techniques, these platforms have successfully reduced QAnon's reach, but these efforts are complicated by QAnon followers' adaptive tactics, such as using coded language and alternative hashtags to avoid detection. Despite these hurdles, tech companies' continuous development of detection tools has helped limit the spread of QAnon on mainstream platforms, even if it hasn't eliminated it completely.

Another promising technological advancement in the fight against QAnon is the use of real-time fact-checking and verification tools. These tools, embedded within social media platforms or accessible through third-party apps, provide users with immediate access to fact-checked information when they encounter potentially misleading content. For example, Facebook and Instagram have begun partnering with independent fact-checking organizations that review flagged posts and provide context or corrections directly on the platform. If a post contains disinformation, users may see a label or link to a reliable source that counters the claim. These fact-checking features are designed to give users the opportunity to question the information they see before accepting it as true, promoting a culture of skepticism and critical thinking. While real-time fact-checking alone may not change the minds of die-hard QAnon followers, it can prevent the casual spread of misinformation to new audiences.

Despite these containment efforts, the evolving nature of technology means that QAnon and similar movements may continue to find new ways to exploit digital tools for dissemination. As technology advances, so do the tactics of disinformation spreaders. Emerging technologies, such as deepfakes, offer new possibilities for creating convincing but entirely false content. A deepfake video of a prominent figure seemingly endorsing QAnon, for example, could quickly gain traction among followers and spread before it can be debunked. To counter this, platforms are investing in detection software that can identify deepfake videos and alert users to their manipulative nature. However, as deepfake technology becomes more sophisticated, the arms race between those spreading disinformation and those attempting to contain it is likely to intensify.

Ultimately, technology's role in amplifying or containing QAnon depends on how it is managed. While digital platforms have empowered QAnon's growth, they also offer tools to limit its spread. The effectiveness of these tools relies on the commitment of tech companies to responsibly manage content and on the public's willingness to critically engage with the information they encounter online. As tech companies continue to refine their moderation techniques and develop new countermeasures, they will need to balance the need for open discourse with the responsibility to protect users from harmful misinformation. Whether technology ultimately serves as an amplifier or a check on QAnon's influence will depend on a complex interplay of digital innovation, regulatory oversight, and collective action by platform users.

4. Ongoing Risks to Society and Public Discourse

The persistence of QAnon and similar conspiracy theories poses significant risks to society, affecting public trust in essential institutions, increasing polarization, and influencing critical social issues. As the movement continues to adapt and attract followers, its reach extends beyond individual beliefs to impact families, communities, and broader public discourse. The ongoing presence of QAnon threatens not only societal cohesion but also democratic stability, as it undermines trust in government, media, healthcare, and other institutions that form the backbone of a functional society.

One of the most profound risks posed by QAnon is the erosion of trust in government and public institutions. QAnon followers frequently view government bodies, law enforcement, healthcare organizations, and educational institutions as part of a corrupt "deep state" working against the public interest. This narrative fosters a fundamental distrust in public officials and experts, which has serious implications for public policy and governance. For example, during the COVID-19 pandemic, QAnon followers and anti-vaccine activists amplified misinformation about vaccines, lockdown measures, and public health guidelines, leading to widespread resistance to health protocols. This distrust in healthcare guidance contributed to lower vaccination rates, putting communities at greater risk and complicating efforts to control the virus. When people reject expertise and proven scientific methods, the collective response to crises becomes fragmented and less effective, leaving society more vulnerable to future challenges.

QAnon's influence on public discourse is also a catalyst for radicalization and social division. Followers of QAnon often believe they are engaged in a righteous struggle against a corrupt elite, a perspective that creates an "us vs. them" mentality. This polarization can lead to increased hostility toward anyone who questions or challenges QAnon beliefs, including family members, friends, and neighbors. Families have reported rifts and estrangement as loved ones become more entrenched in QAnon's worldview, viewing dissenters as part of the problem or as "asleep" to the truth. In communities, this ideological divide weakens the social fabric, making it difficult to have constructive conversations on important topics. As people grow more entrenched in their beliefs and isolate themselves from opposing perspectives, it becomes harder to find common ground, leading to a more polarized and fragmented society.

Public safety is another area where QAnon poses an ongoing risk. The movement's apocalyptic narratives and framing of followers as "digital soldiers" on a mission to save society can inspire acts of violence. For example, several high-profile incidents have shown how individuals influenced by QAnon took dangerous actions, from breaking into federal buildings to confronting perceived enemies. QAnon's claim of a looming battle between good and evil can push followers to adopt extreme behaviors, as they see themselves as agents of change in a corrupt world. The FBI has labeled QAnon a potential domestic terrorism threat, recognizing the risk that the movement's rhetoric can inspire lone actors or small groups to commit violent acts in the name of the conspiracy. As long as QAnon followers view themselves as soldiers in a secret war, the potential for violence remains a pressing concern.

The impact of QAnon extends into critical public issues, shaping how followers approach elections, environmental policies, and social justice movements. QAnon has consistently spread narratives around "rigged elections" and claims of widespread voter fraud, which undermines faith in electoral processes. This distrust is not limited to the United States; as QAnon narratives spread globally, people in other countries have adopted similar beliefs, casting doubt on their own democratic systems. By weakening public faith in elections, QAnon contributes to democratic instability, fostering an environment where people are less likely to accept legitimate outcomes if they do not align with their views. This distrust can lead to lower voter turnout, decreased civic engagement, and the normalization of anti-democratic sentiments, which together erode the foundations of democracy.

Finally, QAnon's influence on individual mental health and family dynamics has broader social consequences. People who become deeply involved in QAnon may experience increased anxiety, isolation, and even paranoia, especially as they perceive hidden threats everywhere. The toll on family relationships can be profound, as family members grapple with the emotional strain of watching loved ones disconnect from reality and become entrenched in conspiracy thinking. Support groups and mental health professionals report a growing need for resources to help families navigate these challenges, highlighting the social cost of QAnon's impact on personal relationships. As people struggle with the effects of disinformation on their loved ones, the collective emotional and psychological toll reverberates across society.

The ongoing risks of QAnon underscore the movement's ability to disrupt societal harmony, weaken democratic structures, and polarize public discourse. While these risks are challenging to address, recognizing the depth of QAnon's impact on society is essential in developing effective responses. By understanding the ways in which QAnon erodes trust, promotes division, and influences behaviors, governments, communities, and individuals can take more informed steps to mitigate these effects, aiming to restore a sense of unity and resilience in the face of disinformation.

5. Strategies for Mitigating QAnon's Impact

To counter the impact of QAnon, society needs a multi-layered approach that addresses the underlying vulnerabilities that make people susceptible to conspiracy theories, as well as practical measures to prevent misinformation from spreading unchecked. Effective strategies require cooperation among governments, tech companies, educational institutions, community organizations, and families. Each has a role to play in building resilience against disinformation, fostering critical thinking, and helping people disengage from harmful beliefs. By addressing the root causes of susceptibility to QAnon, we can build a more informed, united society less prone to divisive, harmful ideologies.

One of the most critical long-term strategies is promoting media literacy and education. Teaching individuals to assess information critically helps create a foundation for resilience against disinformation. Schools, universities, and community programs can play a pivotal role by integrating media literacy into their curricula. Programs that teach people to evaluate sources, recognize bias, and fact-check claims are essential in an era where information is both abundant and easily manipulated. By equipping young people with these skills, educational initiatives foster a generation better prepared to engage thoughtfully with the content they encounter. For older generations who may be less familiar with digital literacy, community-based workshops and resources can help bridge the gap, enabling them to navigate social media and online news with a discerning eye.

Mental health support is another essential strategy in mitigating QAnon's impact, especially for individuals who have become deeply involved in the movement. Conspiracy theories like QAnon often attract people experiencing a sense of loss, disillusionment, or lack of control in their lives. These vulnerabilities can be compounded by isolation, anxiety, or other mental health challenges. Providing mental health resources and support for individuals affected by QAnon, including counseling and support groups, can help them process their beliefs and regain a sense of connection with reality. For family members, understanding the psychological drivers behind conspiracy belief can aid in maintaining open communication and empathy, which are critical in helping loved ones feel supported and understood as they consider leaving the movement.

Community-based programs are also instrumental in addressing QAnon's local impact. Religious institutions, neighborhood organizations, and community leaders are uniquely positioned to reach people in meaningful ways. Grassroots efforts that encourage dialogue, promote accurate information, and foster empathy can help counteract the polarization fueled by QAnon. Community leaders who are trusted by their followers can play a powerful role in challenging QAnon narratives by addressing the fears and anxieties that lead people to embrace conspiracy theories. Community forums and workshops that address misinformation with empathy and respect create safe spaces for individuals to discuss their beliefs without feeling attacked, increasing the chances of meaningful change.

Governments and tech companies also play a vital role in containing the spread of QAnon. Social media platforms have a responsibility to monitor and manage content that promotes harmful conspiracy theories. Algorithms can be adjusted to limit the reach of misinformation, while tools like real-time fact-checking and content labels help users identify false claims. However, moderation must be balanced with protecting freedom of speech. Rather than censorship, platforms can implement transparent policies that prioritize credibility and educate users on how to recognize reliable sources. Governments, in turn, can support these efforts by enacting regulations that encourage transparency in content moderation, protecting users' rights while holding platforms accountable for the spread of harmful content.

Finally, fostering public trust in institutions is essential for counteracting QAnon's influence. QAnon thrives on the erosion of trust in government, media, healthcare, and other pillars of society. To rebuild trust, institutions must prioritize transparency and accountability, especially in areas where public skepticism runs high. Regular, open communication with the public, clear responses to mistakes, and accessible channels for addressing concerns can help bridge the trust gap. For example, public health agencies that maintain open dialogue about their processes, challenges, and successes are more likely to gain the public's confidence. Media outlets that prioritize transparent journalism and avoid sensationalism also contribute to a more informed, trusting public. By making trustworthiness a foundational part of their mission, institutions can weaken the appeal of conspiracy theories by showing people that credible sources can be relied upon.

Mitigating QAnon's impact requires a collective effort and a commitment to addressing the underlying social and psychological factors that fuel its appeal. By combining education, mental health support, community outreach, responsible tech policies, and public trust-building, society can reduce the influence of conspiracy theories and create a more resilient public. These strategies not only help counter QAnon but also protect society against future waves of disinformation, fostering an environment where truth and critical thinking can flourish. In a world increasingly shaped by digital content, building this resilience is essential for safeguarding democracy, promoting social unity, and ensuring that communities can thrive without the divisive forces of conspiracy and mistrust.

Conclusion: The Legacy of QAnon

The rise of QAnon, with its global reach and unrelenting grip on the minds of millions, has left a legacy that will shape society, politics, and digital culture for years to come. What began as cryptic messages on anonymous message boards evolved into one of the most pervasive conspiracy theories of the modern era, with followers spanning every demographic, social class, and national boundary. QAnon has not only challenged our perceptions of truth but has highlighted the vulnerabilities in society that allowed it to flourish. As we consider the long-term impact of QAnon, we are faced with the daunting challenge of de-radicalizing believers and protecting society from future conspiracy movements. This legacy provides a sobering reminder of the power of misinformation and the critical lessons society must absorb in an age marked by hyper-connectivity and deepening political polarization.

1. The Sociopolitical Footprint of QAnon

QAnon's influence on politics and public life cannot be overstated. From the Capitol insurrection on January 6th to its role in shaping perceptions of COVID-19 and vaccine misinformation, QAnon has had far-reaching consequences. Politicians have been elected on platforms that covertly—or overtly—support QAnon beliefs, and the movement's followers have embedded themselves in public discourse, particularly in debates around freedom, governance, and national identity. The theory has fueled distrust in democratic processes, promoting the narrative that elections are rigged and that established institutions are controlled by a hidden cabal. This rhetoric has eroded faith in political systems, with implications for voter turnout, policy debates, and public support for democratic norms.

QAnon's sociopolitical legacy is further reflected in the normalization of conspiracy-based thinking in mainstream politics. By embracing QAnon narratives, some political figures have made conspiratorial thinking a viable part of their platforms, pushing ideas that were once relegated to the fringes into the heart of public debate. This shift has expanded the Overton window, or the range of acceptable political discourse, allowing extreme beliefs to be considered as legitimate perspectives. As QAnon's ideas seep into the political mainstream, they influence the policies and ideologies shaping society, from public health to education. The movement has demonstrated that, in the age of social media, a well-organized and highly motivated minority can exert a profound influence on society's direction.

2. The Challenge of De-radicalizing QAnon Believers

One of the most enduring challenges left in the wake of QAnon is the task of de-radicalizing its followers. Many who became deeply involved in the movement are isolated from friends and family who do not share their beliefs, creating a self-reinforcing echo chamber where skepticism toward the mainstream is strengthened. Unlike traditional cults or radical groups with physical gatherings, QAnon is decentralized and thrives on digital platforms, making it harder to intervene and redirect followers. Many QAnon adherents have built their identity around the movement, viewing themselves as "truth-seekers" engaged in a battle against a corrupt elite. For them, questioning QAnon feels like betraying their purpose, making the process of disengagement not only intellectually challenging but emotionally taxing.

De-radicalization efforts must therefore go beyond simply debunking QAnon's claims. Instead, they require a compassionate approach that acknowledges the psychological and social needs that

QAnon fulfilled for its followers. Mental health support, coupled with educational resources, can provide a foundation for individuals seeking to reconnect with reality. De-radicalization initiatives must also involve family and community support, offering guidance on how to communicate with QAnon believers empathetically, helping them question their beliefs without feeling attacked. It is essential to rebuild a sense of purpose and belonging outside of the movement, allowing former followers to feel understood and valued as they transition away from conspiracy-based thinking.

Furthermore, society needs to recognize the limits of fact-checking in addressing deeply held conspiratorial beliefs. QAnon has illustrated that when a movement becomes a source of identity and belonging, evidence alone cannot dismantle it. De-radicalization must be multifaceted, integrating mental health approaches with community engagement and tailored interventions that address the unique motivations behind each individual's belief in QAnon. The challenge is immense, but developing and refining these approaches is essential, not only for those affected by QAnon but also for the prevention of future movements built on similar ideologies.

3. Lessons on the Power of Hyper-Connectivity and Misinformation

QAnon has provided a stark lesson on the influence of hyper-connectivity in modern society. The internet has enabled individuals to connect across vast distances, forming communities and alliances that would have been unimaginable just a few decades ago. For QAnon, this connectivity was a powerful tool that allowed the movement to rapidly grow, evolve, and adapt to new circumstances. The decentralized nature of the internet allowed followers to evade traditional gatekeepers of information—such as media outlets, government institutions, and academic experts—while creating their own, self-sustaining sources of authority. The lesson is clear: in an interconnected world, misinformation can spread with unprecedented speed and scope, reaching millions before fact-checkers or regulators have a chance to intervene.

This hyper-connectivity has also given rise to new methods of influence and control, such as algorithms that prioritize sensational content and create echo chambers. Social media platforms have inadvertently fostered a culture of misinformation by prioritizing engagement over accuracy, promoting posts that drive user interaction, regardless of their veracity. In many cases, QAnon's growth was fueled by platforms that rewarded engagement, allowing the movement to gain traction through algorithmic amplification. This lesson underscores the need for tech companies to take responsibility for the information they disseminate, as well as the importance of developing and refining algorithms that can limit the spread of harmful content without stifling freedom of expression.

Additionally, QAnon highlights the challenge of misinformation in the age of anonymity. On message boards, forums, and social media, users can post without revealing their identity, creating a breeding ground for unaccountable information. Anonymous posting has allowed QAnon's "Q" figure to become a trusted source without followers ever knowing the person's identity or credibility. This culture of anonymity complicates accountability and promotes a level of trust in unseen authorities, opening the door for figures who may have ulterior motives to sway public opinion. Moving forward, society must grapple with the tension between online anonymity as a tool for free expression and its potential to amplify harmful ideologies.

4. The Lasting Influence on Conspiracy Culture

QAnon has not only left an immediate impact but also a template for future conspiracy theories. The movement's tactics and strategies—cryptic messages, decentralized communities, and an evolving narrative—have set a new standard for conspiracy culture. QAnon has shown that followers don't need a clear leader; they need a compelling narrative that allows them to feel part of a larger cause. Future movements may adopt QAnon's "do your own research" mentality, encouraging followers to interpret ambiguous clues and build their own narratives, which fosters a sense of ownership and engagement that makes conspiracies hard to dismantle.

QAnon has also introduced a degree of permanence to certain conspiracy themes. Ideas like the "deep state," elite child trafficking rings, and the notion of a hidden cabal of powerful figures have become embedded in the public psyche. These concepts may reappear in future movements, as they appeal to deep-rooted fears of corruption and manipulation by those in power. QAnon's legacy ensures that even if the movement itself fades, its core ideas will remain, ready to be repurposed by future conspiracy theorists.

5. Building a Resilient Society

Ultimately, the legacy of QAnon is a call to action for building a society resilient to disinformation and conspiracy theories. The response to QAnon must go beyond containment and instead address the social, psychological, and structural factors that made the movement so successful. Media literacy programs must be a priority, equipping individuals with the skills to critically evaluate information. By teaching people to question sources, recognize manipulation tactics, and understand bias, society can foster a culture of informed skepticism that resists the appeal of misinformation.

Public trust in institutions must also be restored, as mistrust was a key driver behind QAnon's success. Government transparency, corporate accountability, and honest communication from media outlets are essential to building a society that trusts its foundational institutions. When people feel that they can rely on those in power, they are less likely to seek alternative explanations in conspiracies. Transparency in government actions, openness to public scrutiny, and respect for diverse voices can help rebuild this trust, creating a society where individuals feel informed rather than deceived.

Finally, mental health resources and community-based support are vital for addressing the psychological needs that often lead people to conspiracy theories. Many QAnon followers joined the movement seeking answers, purpose, or belonging, underscoring the importance of addressing the root causes of alienation and isolation. By providing mental health resources and community support, society can offer meaningful alternatives to the promises of conspiracy theories, allowing individuals to find fulfillment outside of misinformation-driven movements.

Conclusion

The legacy of QAnon is complex, presenting both a cautionary tale and an opportunity for growth. It has underscored the dangers of unchecked misinformation and the urgent need for society to address the conditions that allow conspiracy theories to flourish. Through a combination of media literacy, trust-building, mental health support, and technological responsibility, we can work toward a more informed and resilient society—one less vulnerable to the allure of QAnon and the divisive, destructive power of conspiracy theories. QAnon's rise has revealed our collective vulnerabilities, but in addressing its legacy, we have the chance to build a stronger, more unified future.

Appendix: Glossary of Terms and Key Figures

This glossary provides definitions for key terms and figures within the QAnon movement, helping readers understand the concepts, language, and individuals central to QAnon's narrative. These definitions highlight how specific terms and people contributed to QAnon's evolution and the movement's impact on followers.

Key Terms

- **Q**

  The anonymous figure believed to be the source of the QAnon movement's information. Q is said to have high-level security clearance within the U.S. government, allegedly sharing inside knowledge about secret operations against a global "cabal" of elites. Q's identity remains unknown, and followers continue to view Q's messages as authoritative.

- **Q Drops**

  Cryptic messages posted by Q on anonymous message boards (initially on 4chan and later on 8kun). These drops often contain phrases, clues, or coded language, prompting followers to interpret the information and build their own theories. Q drops are central to QAnon, as followers view them as insider information revealing hidden truths about the government and world events.

- **The Storm**

  A significant QAnon concept predicting a day when prominent members of the "cabal" will be arrested en masse, leading to a public revelation of their crimes. "The Storm" represents a climactic event where QAnon followers believe justice will be served, with widespread societal and political ramifications. This term was inspired by Donald Trump's 2017 comment about "the calm before the storm" during a photo-op with military leaders.

- **The Great Awakening**

  A QAnon concept describing a future period when the general public becomes aware of the "truth" about the alleged cabal and its influence. The Great Awakening refers to a societal shift where followers believe people will recognize and reject the elites' control over society, bringing about a new era of transparency and justice.

- **The Cabal**

  In QAnon terminology, the cabal refers to a hidden group of powerful elites allegedly involved in criminal activities, including child trafficking and political corruption. Followers believe that this cabal includes prominent politicians, business leaders, Hollywood figures, and international organizations working to control society and undermine democratic values.

- **Deep State**

  A term used to describe the network of bureaucrats, intelligence officials, and influential figures who QAnon followers believe secretly control government operations and actively work against the interests of the public. In QAnon's narrative, the deep state is an obstacle that Donald Trump and QAnon followers must dismantle.

- **Red-Pilling**

  Borrowed from *The Matrix* film, red-pilling describes the process of awakening someone to the "truth" as perceived by QAnon followers. Red-pilling is used to describe how individuals come to understand QAnon's worldview, often through online research and exposure to conspiracy theories.

- **Bread Crumbs**

Small pieces of information that QAnon followers interpret and connect to larger theories. Q often leaves these "bread crumbs" in Q drops, encouraging followers to do their own research and build narratives that connect seemingly unrelated events to QAnon's worldview.

- **Digital Soldiers**

A term used by QAnon followers to describe their role in the movement. Digital soldiers view themselves as part of an online army fighting to spread the truth, protect society from the cabal, and expose alleged conspiracies. They actively share, research, and create content to awaken others to QAnon's beliefs.

- **Save the Children**

Originally a legitimate charity campaign, this phrase was adopted by QAnon followers to spread the belief that a global child trafficking network, run by elites, is operating in secrecy. The phrase became a rallying cry for QAnon adherents, who view child protection as a central goal of the movement, although no evidence supports the existence of such a network.

- **Do Your Own Research (DYOR)**

A central tenet of QAnon, this phrase encourages followers to independently investigate Q's claims rather than relying on mainstream sources. DYOR reinforces the idea that QAnon followers are uncovering hidden truths by connecting disparate pieces of information themselves.

- **WWG1WGA (Where We Go One, We Go All)**

A slogan adopted by QAnon followers, symbolizing unity and loyalty within the movement. The phrase is used to express solidarity and commitment to the QAnon cause, and it frequently appears in social media posts and on QAnon-related merchandise.

- **False Flags**

  Events that QAnon followers believe are staged or manipulated to mislead the public. In the QAnon narrative, false flags are often used by the deep state to distract from their activities or to manipulate public opinion. Followers interpret various tragedies, such as mass shootings, as possible false flags orchestrated to achieve a hidden agenda.

- **Trust the Plan**

  A phrase used by QAnon followers to maintain faith in Q's mission, despite unfulfilled predictions or external criticism. This motto encourages followers to stay patient and believe that "the plan" will eventually succeed in exposing and dismantling the cabal.

Key Figures

- **Donald Trump**

  The former U.S. president is seen as a central hero in the QAnon narrative. Followers believe that Trump was working behind the scenes to fight the deep state and protect society from the cabal. QAnon theories often portray Trump as a figure who, alongside Q, orchestrates a secret plan to expose and punish corrupt elites.

- **Michael Flynn**

  Former National Security Advisor and retired general, Flynn is viewed as a supporter of QAnon after he publicly endorsed the movement and took the QAnon "oath." His legal battles and vocal opposition to the "deep state" have made him a prominent figure among followers, who see him as a patriot committed to exposing government corruption.

- **Ron Watkins**

  A former administrator of 8kun, the message board where Q posted, Watkins is suspected by some researchers to be one of the people behind the Q identity. Known for his involvement in spreading conspiracy theories, Watkins has become a significant influencer in the QAnon community, particularly regarding claims of election fraud.

- **Jim Watkins**

  Owner of 8kun and father of Ron Watkins, Jim is another individual suspected of being involved in QAnon's development. He has been outspoken in supporting the movement and has allowed QAnon content to thrive on his platform. His role in enabling QAnon has made him a central figure in discussions about the movement's origins.

- **Sidney Powell**

  An attorney associated with QAnon after her involvement in cases challenging the 2020 U.S. election results, Powell has been a vocal proponent of the "deep state" theory and claims of widespread election fraud. Her public statements about secret plots and corruption have reinforced QAnon's beliefs among followers.

- **Lin Wood**

  A lawyer and prominent figure in conservative circles, Wood gained popularity within the QAnon community after making claims of election fraud and corruption among government officials. His outspoken support for QAnon theories has made him a polarizing figure, both within the legal community and among followers.

- **Marjorie Taylor Greene**

  A U.S. Congresswoman and early supporter of QAnon, Greene has expressed support for the movement and has shared QAnon-related ideas on social media. Her election to

Congress and high-profile statements have brought QAnon beliefs into the mainstream, increasing the movement's visibility and influence.

- **"Anons"**

  Short for "anonymous," Anons are the followers of QAnon who actively engage in Q's messages, conduct their own research, and spread QAnon theories online. Anons are instrumental in QAnon's growth, as they create content, develop narratives, and reinforce the movement's beliefs across various digital platforms.

- **Joe M**

  A prominent QAnon influencer known for creating videos and social media content that explain and promote Q's messages. Joe M's media production helped to popularize QAnon ideas among followers and new audiences alike, contributing significantly to QAnon's online growth.

This glossary highlights the central language, symbols, and individuals that define QAnon's worldview and appeal. Each term and figure represents a crucial piece of the QAnon narrative, which has reshaped modern conspiracy culture and revealed the potency of digital communities in spreading and sustaining alternative belief systems. The glossary provides context for understanding how these elements work together to create a movement that has captivated millions and left an indelible mark on public discourse.